The Education of Human Ecologists

The Education of Human Ecologists

*The proceedings of a Symposium
held at The Polytechnic, Huddersfield
28-29 March 1972*

EDITED BY PAUL ROGERS

1972
CHARLES KNIGHT & CO LTD
London

Charles Knight & Co. Ltd.
11/12 Bury Street, London EC3A 5AP
Dowgate Works, Douglas Road, Tonbridge, Kent

First published 1973

ISBN 0 85314 174 6

Printed in Great Britain by
List and Print Services Ltd.,
a member of the Brown Knight & Truscott Group
London and Tonbridge.

Contents

Foreword

Concern with the problems of the human environment has led to an increased interest in the teaching of human environment studies to students at all levels. At the present time major changes are taking place in universities and polytechnics in this field with the development of a number of multi-disciplinary courses, all concerned with a study of aspects of the human environment.

As often happens in a rapidly changing situation, there has been a tendency for these developments to take place in isolation and the present publication is a record of a symposium held early in 1972 which attempted to break down this isolation and allow an exchange of information and views.

The symposium was called "The Education of Human Ecologists", the term human ecologist being used because it is becoming increasingly synonymous with "human environment studies". It was organised by the Huddersfield Polytechnic in association with the Commonwealth Human Ecology Council and was attended by ninety participants from universities, Polytechnics, schools, industry and local and national government. Sixteen papers were presented and these were grouped into three sessions, an arrangement which has been retained for this publication.

PART 1

In the first session, three papers considered the nature of human ecology and its political and commercial contexts. Dr. Barton Worthington, Scientific Director of the International Biological Programme, gave the first paper in which he discussed the meaning and scope of the term human ecology and this was followed by a paper by Professor Gerald Fowler on the political context. Professor Fowler is Professor of Educational Administration at the Open University and was formerly Minister of State in the Department of Education and Science. Finally, Barry Gregson-Allcott, Education Secretary of the Institute of Biology, discussed present and future employment prospects for graduates in human ecology.

PART 2

The second session considered the contributions to human ecology of the principal disciplines concerned in the study of the human environment.

In all, six papers were presented in this session commencing with the contribution of Ecology discussed by Professor Palmer Newbould of the Department of Biology, New University of Ulster. Following this Economics was considered by Alan Petch, Senior Lecturer in Economics at the University of Newcastle, and then Geography, discussed by Professor Howard Bowen-Jones, Director of the Institute of Middle Eastern and Islamic Studies at the University of Durham.

A paper on Anthropology was presented by Dr. V. G. Sheddick, Professor of Social Organisation at the New University of Ulster and this was followed by a paper discussing the contribution of the physical design professions given by Michael Lloyd of Land Use Consultants, formerly Principal of the Architectural Association. The final paper of the session was on the role of Medical Science and was presented by Dr. D. R. Hannay of the Department of Epidemiology and Preventive Medicine at Glasgow University.

PART 3

The final session was devoted to papers describing courses already in progress or under development. Of the seven papers presented, one was concerned with secondary education serving as a basis for discussing six new degree courses, four in universities and two in polytechnics.

Sean Carson, Adviser on Environmental Education for Hertfordshire County Council presented the first paper which described the new 'A' level syllabus on "Environmental Studies" being developed in schools in Hertfordshire.

The six degree courses which were then described provide a wide range of approaches to the study of the human environment. At the University of Aston in Birmingham a course on "The Biology of Man and His Environment" has been in operation for five years as part of the Combined Honours Programme at Aston. It adopts a biological approach and was described by Professor A. J. Matty of the Department of Biological Sciences at Aston. The degree programme in Environmental Sciences at the University of East Anglia adopts a rather more geographical approach, discussed here by Dr. J. R. Tarrant of the School of Environmental Sciences at UEA.

At Oxford the Honour School in Human Sciences is concerned primarily with biological and social aspects of the study of man and was described by Mr. E. Paget of the Department of Geography at Oxford. The fourth of the university degree courses considered here is the Technological Economics (Biology) course at the University of Stirling where the emphasis is on management economics and industrial science in relation to biology. The paper was given by Professor F. R. Bradbury of the

Department of Industrial Science at Stirling who, while refraining from describing a graduate of this course as a human ecologist, would expect him to make significant contributions to solving many human ecology problems.

The two polytechnic degree courses are both courses still under development. In fact, the first of the papers described three courses, all under development at Plymouth Polytechnic and all closely concerned with human environment studies. It was presented by Dr. Leonard Heath, Head of the Department of Environmental Sciences at Plymouth. The second paper, by Ralph Eden, Senior Lecturer in charge of Biology at Huddersfield Polytechnic, concluded the contributions with a description of the Human Ecology degree course under development at Huddersfield.

DISCUSSION

Summaries of the discussions following the papers at the symposium are given in these proceedings, but in addition to the general discussion, workshop sessions were arranged in which participants had an opportunity for more detailed discussion of points raised during the symposium. The main points arising from these group discussions are given in the conclusion to these proceedings. They are of particular interest in that they extend over the whole field of environmental education and are not restricted to higher and further education, the main area covered by the formal papers.

Paul Rogers
May 1972   The Polytechnic, Huddersfield

Part 1

Human Ecology and Society

Introductory Address

K. J. DURRANDS

Rector

Huddersfield Polytechnic

I would like to welcome you to Huddersfield and to this Polytechnic on the occasion of our first symposium on human ecology. I am particularly pleased to welcome four distinguished guests, Mrs Zena Daysh, Secretary-General of the Commonwealth Human Ecology Council; Dr Jan Cerovsky, Education Commission Executive of the International Union for the Conservation of Nature; Mr J Owen Jones, Director of the Commonwealth Bureau of Agricultural Economics and Mr J Eedle, Senior Education Officer with the Commonwealth Secretariat.

I would suggest that there are a number of reasons for organising this symposium at the present time. First, perhaps obviously, the study of the human environment is at last starting to receive the attention it merits and this has led to the realisation that there are very few people adequately educated for this study. As a result a number of novel courses are now under development in universities and polytechnics and we will have an opportunity to examine many of these over the next few days.

Secondly, the Polytechnic has developed a major interest in human environment studies. Situated as we are in an area of diverse and long-standing industrial activity, examples of virtually every environmental problem arising from urbanisation and industrialisation are to be found within a few miles of here. We have even received enquiries from institutes located in more comfortable parts of the country, seeking to bring students here on field courses in order to show them the environmental problems now being faced. Several local areas are now the subjects of research projects being undertaken within the Polytechnic and we run a number of courses concerned with human environment problems. On an historical note, the Polytechnic is proud of its association with the late Dr Thomas Woodhead, one time head of the Biology Department, a founder member of the British Ecological Society and indeed one of the founders of ecology in Britain.

Finally we have a close working relationship with the Common-wealth Human Ecology Council and were, in fact, the first institute in the Commonwealth to apply for membership of the Council. We are anxious to further the work of the Council and I would like to take this opportunity of thanking the staff of the Council, especially Mrs Daysh, for their help in organising this symposium.

As well as these general reasons for holding this symposium I would like to exercise the chairman's prerogative and add a personal note, from two points of view; one as someone fortunate to have been brought up in a small village and to witness some of the major changes that have taken place in agriculture and the other as an engineer.

I can still remember the time in 1938 when the first tractor came to the village where I lived to replace a number of horses. At that time some of the old and experienced farmers and farm workers said the machine was too heavy and would compact and ruin the soil. Thirty years later the government thought it necessary to institute a de-tailed study of soil deterioration problems, largely brought about by farm mechanisation! I can remember these men saying that the advent of widespread use of pesticide sprays and the general removal of hedges and trees would have a catastrophic effect on wildlife. Again they have been proved right. And I can recall the scepticism with which the advent of antibiotic additives in animal feed was met, a practice which is meeting increasing opposition. These were men with little formal education but a wealth of experience, a fact worth re-membering in discussions on formal education courses.

In engineering we have been concerned for many years about the effects of our work on the environment but many of us find ourselves controlled by price factors which prevent us from ensuring that the plants we build are environmentally acceptable.

The scale of pollution from new plants can be very large indeed. Take, for example, a fossil-fuelled power station producing 2,000 megawatts per 24 hours. This station will burn 17,800 tons of coal in those twenty-four hours and use 34,000 tons of air, producing in turn 693 tons of sulphur dioxide. Such a station will cost something in the region of £100 m. but it would require several more million pounds to render it pollution-free.

Let me come on to the nuclear power station which the layman marvels at, seeing no chimneys and therefore thinking there is no effluent. For the production of one megawatt-day of heat by nuclear fission, 1 gram of uranium is turned into 1 gram of fission products. Our present 6,000 megawatts of nuclear power capacity will require about 6 million megawatt-days of nuclear heat yearly so that the rate of production of fission products will be about 6 million grams (or 6 tons) a year. The specific activity of the fission products will be about 1,700 curies per gram one day after removal from the reactor falling to one half in 100 days. The total amount of activity brought into existence each year is therefore measured in thousands of millions of curies.

Hazards can, of course, only arise if this material gets out of control, but not very much need get out of control to create a serious hazard. Thus breathing air contaminated to the extent of one hundredth of a curie per cubic metre for a couple of hours would have serious consequences, while ground contaminated to the extent of one hundredth of a curie per square metre would have to be evacuated. The mismatch between what can be tolerated and what will be created is thus extremely large, and we can see that even supposedly clean nuclear power stations produce wastes which pose major problems for disposal.

As engineers, many of us can only wonder at a society which calls upon us to build plants which pollute our streams and rivers and also to build more plants to purify the polluted water in order to make it potable. You can imagine then that as an engineer I welcome this symposium as a potential contribution to ensuring that society will enable us to carry out our work with due regard to environmental considerations.

I will make no attempt to define human ecology at this stage. There will be plenty of scope for that during the symposium. I will, however, indicate the structure of the symposium.

In this introductory session we will have an opportunity to consider the nature of human ecology and its development within the context of political and commercial trends in this country. Following that, a series of papers will be presented which will discuss the contribution which a number of disciplines can make to human ecology. In the third session we will learn of the progress made in the development of a number of courses concerned with the study of the human environment, and this will lead on to the final session when the symposium will divide into small groups to give participants an opportunity to discuss, in depth, the views expressed at the symposium. A short plenary session will attempt a summary of this discussion.

1

What is Human Ecology?

E. BARTON WORTHINGTON

The organiser of this symposium has sent me details of several University Degree Courses related to Human Ecology. In studying these, I came to the conclusion that I should not be standing here trying to answer the question "What is Human Ecology?" but I should be going back to school. However, without the advantage of having attended these courses I am committed to attempting the question, so here goes.

First we must consider what Ecology is without the human epithet. One thing which Ecology is *not*, but many writers and speakers on the subject seem to think it is, is a kind of receptacle into which one can throw all the sense, and a lot of the nonsense, about the environment, pollution, conservation, contraception, and a whole lot of other subjects which have some bearing on what is referred to as the Predicament of Man or the Environmental Crisis. These form the ingredients of the witches' cauldron which is presided over by the Doom-Watchers. I declare straightway that I do not number myself among the Doom-Watchers, nor among those who appear to assume that everything will be "alright on the night". I subscribe to the view that if present trends of population growth and consumption of resources were to continue, disaster would overcome the human species. Therefore it is extremely important to ensure that present trends do not continue; and hence the importance of education in human ecology.

The term ecology, which until a few years ago implied a reasonably discrete and definable branch of the biological sciences, has rather suddenly come to be used for an ill-defined but highly varied group of subjects which, if only we could understand them and their processes, would provide solutions to many problems currently facing the world.

The term ecology has, in fact, been abused. I met an extreme form of abuse last year attending a conference on the University Campus of Tennessee, when I saw a notice calling a meeting on the Ecology of Newspapers. This looked interesting from the sociological point of view so I went to the meeting only to discover that it was to organise gangs of students to tidy up the Campus by collecting all the thrown-away news-papers. Ecologists deeply deplore the looseness, if not meaninglessness, with which their subject is now banded about, so let's look at what it really means. The derivation is simple enough, "oikos" means a house or habitation, and "logos" means the word or study. So ecology came to be used by biologists early in this century for the study of the organism (plant or animal) in relation to its environment. Ecology was developed into a scientific discipline involving defined methods of research first by botanists, and the fact that ecology is a rather recent development in biology is witnessed by the fact that some of the scientists who started it are still alive today — Sir Edward Salisbury, former Director of Kew, for example.

Plant Ecology got itself recognised between the two wars but it was a longish time before the number of its exponents could be numbered in hundreds rather than in tens. Animal Ecology was later and more difficult, for the obvious reason that animals will not stay put so they are More difficult than plants to study in relation to the environment. Charles Elton of Oxford, who is still an active researcher, is recognised as one of the main originators of Animal Ecology and I hope that his excellent small book on the subject, written in the twenties, will continue to be standard reading for university students for many a long year to come.

Whatever organisms we are primarily interested in, the study of ecology in nature (including man-made nature) involves a process of analysis — a breaking down of the situation into its component parts and their separate examination — followed by a process of synthesis in which the structure of the situation is pieced together into a meaningful whole. Both in the analysis and the synthesis, several scientific disciplines are generally involved so the subject tends to become interdisciplinary. Ecology in fact tends to be divided into many branches such as population ecology, genetical ecology, behavioural ecology. I suggest, however that for our present purposes it is convenient to split it into two branches only, autecology and synecology. Autecology considers a particular species as the centrepiece of a complex, surrounded by the components of the environment — the physical environment of climate, soil and water, and the biological environment of all living things. Synecology on the other hand, looks at the total complex and at all the species of plants and animals equally with the factors of the environment; it slots each species into its "ecological niche", and thereby pieces together the jigsaw puzzle of the total ecosystem.

By the very fact of adding the adjective "human" in front of "ecology", we are thinking in terms of autecology rather than synecology. We are bringing the human species into special focus as the centrepiece. Our purpose is to understand the effect of the environment on mankind, and the effect of mankind on the environment — and also the influences of men and women on each other — whether widely scattered in a rural setting or crowded together in towns.

What then should we include within the subject of human ecology? First think of the effects of the environment on mankind: to encompass these we must include human biology and physiology, the reactions and adaptations of the human body to the great variety of conditions in which it can live, high temperatures and low temperatures, high altitudes and low altitudes, high latitudes and low latitudes. We can live in extremely dry air and at the opposite end we can live almost submerged in water. Human ecology must include man's capacity for work and play in such contrasting conditions, his needs for food, clothing and shelter; the diseases and ills from which he suffers; his population dynamics and breeding habits.

Now consider the effects of man on his environment. There has been a tendency in recent years to emphasise the bad effects rather than the good, the degradation rather than the improvement in the environment. But consider the rural scene in Britain, which many of us think of as a beautiful and satisfying environment — it is almost entirely man-made. Compare the uniformity and monotony of the forest clad hills of England before man and his impact, with the diversity of today's patchwork countryside of field, coppice, village and common. Whether in relation to the productivity of farming, the diversity of habitat for wildlife, or just aesthetic beauty, there is no question that the influence of mankind has been to advantage.

Go overseas, to Africa for example, and see the influence of fire on the broad savannah lands, still inhabited in national parks by thirty or forty different species of large mammals which need the fire-created space and cannot support life under the stranglehold of thickets to which much of this land reverts in the rare cases where fire is excluded. I do not say that burning the land is always good — obviously it is wasteful of organic production — but in the present stages of land use over much of the tropical lands it is a necessary form of land use, and under appropriate controls can improve the environment.

Of course there have been many mistakes in man's use of land, water and air; some of them have resulted in pollution in one form or another which is proving extremely expensive to overcome. However, in almost no case are anti-pollution measures impossible, as witnessed by the recent improvement in London's air and London's river. Sometimes more serious than pollution is the over-use of land resulting from increasing pressure which leads to the degradation of ecosystems — the degradation, for instance, from forest to savannah, savannah to grassland, grassland to desert, all of which processes are extremely difficult to reverse. The systems of land use which lead to such degradation are not necessarily bad in themselves: shifting cultivation and pastoralism are good methods of arable agriculture and animal industry respectively in tropical woodlands and grasslands, provided there is plenty of land to go around. But the impact of modern medicine in reducing death rates before the socioeconomic system has had time to readjust balances, has made sure that there is no longer enough land to go round. The resulting degradation has had very serious effects on productivity over wide areas.

Such considerations lead on to perhaps the biggest effect of all of mankind on his environment, through the sheer weight of numbers in some localities. Obviously this is most pronounced in towns which a high proportion of our species prefer to the rural environment (for reasons which I personally find difficulty in understanding). Human urban ecology is, in fact, a subject very different from human rural ecology. Here again mistakes have been made, many of them obvious in the light of hindsight. But in Europe at least, if one compares the average conditions of living in towns today with a generation or two ago, it is quite astonishing to tot up the improvements made by man and his technology, in spite of the ever-growing complexity of the problem.

Let us now break down the habitat of man into some of its component parts and see how they relate to each other. In doing so we can bear in mind two concepts of ecology, first the food-chain or food-web, and second the flow of energy through the ecosystem. The accompanying diagram of relationships (which are applicable more to the rural setting than the urban setting) could be elaborated into a food-web by putting in the individual species of plants, animals etc., and the races of human beings. The arrows indicate some of the main channels through which energy flows through an ecosystem, as one form of inorganic or organic matter changes into another.

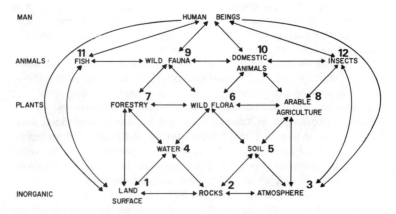

RURAL MAN AND HIS ENVIRONMENT

Thus we start with the configuration of the land (1), the rocks of which it is comprised (2), and the atmosphere above it (3). These three subjects, constituting the physical basis of the environment, determine that all important factor — water supply (4). The interaction of ground structure, climate and water is responsible for the character of the soil (5) which, acting as a link between the inorganic and the organic, brings us to the group of subjects which constitute plant-life. The soil determines and is determined by the flora growing upon it (6) and from this point we proceed to an applied branch of botanical science, namely forestry (7) and to arable agriculture or plant industry (8). Rising from the level of primary producers (plants) to consumers (animals) we have the categories of wild animals (9) and domestic animals (10). Then to the left the study of water-life and its applied subject of fisheries (11), and on the right insects (12), especially (as affecting human ecology) those which are pests or vectors of disease. Thus we reach the climax of man himself (13) which, being the centrepiece in human ecology, should have reversible arrows to all other subjects in the diagram.

Concerning the flow of energy through the ecosystem it is well to remember that only a tiny proportion of its original source — radiation from the sun — as received at the earth's surface, is actually used in plant growth. In those plant associations whose ecosystem physiology has been studied — (a special assessment was made for instance of an area of perennial grassland vegetation in Michigan) it transpires that, of the total solar energy incident upon the vegetation, nearly 99% is lost through reflection or used in evaporation, and of the remaining 1% which is turned into gross primary production through photosynthesis and carbon assimilation, there is some further loss of energy through plant respiration. Although different types of terrestrial and aquatic ecosystems will clearly produce differences in the equation, it does not seem that many of them will prove to be much more efficient than this.

When you consider the large proportion of the terrestrial world, such as deserts and snowfields — where there is no vegetation to speak of, and the much larger areas of ocean where the lack of nutrients in solution severely limits the use of sunlight for photosynthesis, the total of the sun's energy actually used in the creation of biological resources is far less than 1%. For practical purposes all the rest goes to waste and one cannot help feeling a hunch that some brilliant technologist will sooner or later find a way of catching it before our finite energy resources of oil, coal and nuclear fuel approach the exhaustion point.

But that is a sideline of conjecture. Passing from the primary producers to the secondary producers, there is further loss of energy, for herbivores do not assimilate anything like all of the food which they consume. As much as 90% of the food intake may pass out of the body as faeces and not all of the balance goes into building animal tissue, because there are further energy losses through movement, respiration, reproduction and keeping warm in homo-thermous animals. In carnivores, as tertiary producers, a higher proportion of the food eaten is assimilated — probably between 30 and 75% — but the losses through energy consumption and searching for food are generally higher than in herbivores.

We should not forget that the apparent great loss of energy through faeces of both herbivores and carnivores is not lost to the ecosystem, for the faeces together with the body tissues of the plants and animals, serve as food material for other animals and bacteria and fungi before being recycled through the soil. At each transfer of energy, heat is evolved, the end point being such that solar energy entering the ecosystem equals the energy leaving it.

Coming back to the teaching of human ecology I think that a simple diagram of subject relationships such as I have sketched can be a starting point, and from the diversity of disciplines which are mentioned in the various university teaching curricula it would seem that this is well recognised. I notice by the way that only one university, the New University of Ulster, attempts in its curriculum to define Human Ecology. They call it "the study of the complex of interrelationships whereby human populations coexist with other species in the physical context of nature". As a biologist I would go along with this, for I think that the essential biological nature of ecology is sometimes forgotten by those who talk about it. In this connection I would quote Professor Borgstrom from the Observer, 5th March, recording an important discussion between him, Dr. Borlaug and Gerald Leech, "the urbanised millions of America and Europe have almost entirely lost touch with the complex biological forces and restraints that make life on this planet tick. I think this loss of biological understanding was really the starting point of our ecological crisis".

This brings me to a final comment which concerns the behaviour and hence the ecology of the human species as well as all other living organisms. I would draw attention to the two great urges towards the survival of the individual and the survival of the race. We can perhaps think of them as the urge towards "hunger" and the urge towards "love". The two sometimes get mixed up, but in the human species included under "hunger" come most of the direct relationships between man and his environment — his dependence on food gathering, hunting, agriculture, industry or other activities which lead not only to individual survival, but to personal aggrandisement (property rights and money) as exhibited by the rat race in modern society. On the other hand "love" in this context is responsible not only for reproductive behaviour, but for family and group contacts and linkages. From the "love" urge comes many sublimations, for example in music and the arts, religion and philanthropy.

Until the last generation or two the human species in common with all other animal species was not nearing the limits of its resources, so hunger and love could be allowed full play. But latterly, as we are currently reminded in nearly every newspaper, human exercise of these two urges has been so successful that both the survival of the individual and the survival of the race are outrunning what is reasonable and indeed have come into conflict with each other. The population of our species has set itself on a collision course with the natural resources on which it depends. The possible consequences of this and how they might be averted or at least ameliorated, is also part of human ecology.

Discussion

E. Paget, Oxford University. I am glad to see that we intend to examine the nature of the discipline of human ecology. On reading through the papers to be presented at this symposium I wonder whether the breadth of study is too great and whether the accuracy and academic respectability of the discipline will not suffer as a result.

H. Roper, Liverpool Polytechnic. It is unfortunate that there are so few planners present because the subject under discussion is one of increasing interest to the planning profession. With regard to Dr. Worthington's paper I have one question. Is it not true that man's behaviour in response to his environment is very much conditioned by his psychical make-up? I would therefore have thought that psychologists have a contribution to make to human ecology.

E. B. Worthington. While agreeing with that remark I would just comment that there is a danger in bringing in too great a breadth of study at the undergraduate level. Behavioural aspects of human ecology might best be studied, in depth, at the postgraduate level.

Dr. D. R. Hannay, Glasgow University. I would support Mr. Roper in wishing to see the behavioural sciences playing a major role in human ecology. On another point, I wonder just how helpful it is to speak in terms of urban and rural ecology when discussing human ecology. There does not seem to be a definite division between the two.

Dr. D. Kirby, Huddersfield Polytechnic. It is worth remembering that decision making is undertaken not only in terms of the general environment, but in terms of the environment as it is perceived by the decision-maker. This surely brings behavioural sciences right in with ecology, architecture, planning and all the other disciplines concerned with the human environment.

E. B. Worthington. Although I am in sympathy with that view I must repeat my concern that, at least at the undergraduate level, we must be careful to avoid making the study of human ecology too nebulous and broad.

Dr. J. R. Tarrant, University of East Anglia. To return to Dr. Hannay's comment, I too would question the distinction between urban and rural ecology. Although western man is predominantly a town dweller, I do not think a hard distinction can any longer be made.

E. B. Worthington. If we are to approach the study of the human environment in a scientific manner, the process of analysis must precede synthesis. Several human ecological studies, e.g. the International Biological Programme studies on eskimoes and also on pygmies have been concerned with rural populations, but it is becoming accepted that urban man is tending to behave in ways different from his rural counterparts.

D. R. Hannay. Are you an urban or a rural man? I understand that although you live in rural Sussex, you work in urban London.

E. B. Worthington. That's true, but only because I have to!

Dr. G. S. Puri, Liverpool Polytechnic. I would support Dr. Worthington's distinction, remembering that we are by no means concerned just with western man; in the tropics, man remains in largely rural habitats.

E. B. Worthington. We tend, in western countries, to be concerned predominantly with urban studies and forget that in Africa, for example, more than 80% of people live in rural areas. I suspect that Lord Pearce would have had an easier job in Rhodesia if he had started with the rural majority instead of the urban minority!

P. Carter, Bristol Polytechnic. On a more general point I rather resent the common implication that biologists, and especially ecologists, are the only people competent to express opinions on environmental matters. There are many people who have not had the benefit of formal training in these fields who are well aware that we are all part of the world ecosystem. With regard to the education of human ecologists, the other disciplines mentioned during this discussion are all important and should be developed continually with the fundamental ecological approach.

E. B. Worthington. We need a continuing debate involving all these disciplines, but whether we could maintain that a broadened approach to human ecology could still use the term "ecology" is another question, although perhaps just a matter of semantics.

2
The Political Context

G. T. FOWLER

I am not a geographer, a biologist, a planner, or an expert in any of the academic disciplines which may be thought to contribute to the study of human ecology. I am not even a politician at this moment of time, although I am a past and I trust a future politician. My only claim therefore to speak on this subject to-day is that I am at this moment without *parti pris*. Nor, I should make it clear at the outset, do I hold a "doomwatch" philosophy; I believe that if the community as a whole, through the organs of government, and taking the best advice available to it from time to time, takes the requisite action then all is not lost for humankind. It should however here be stressed that the "community" means not only this and other particular national communities, but also the international community, since many of the environmental problems which we face are international or even on a world scale.

Perhaps the most important question on both a national and international level for the politician as opposed to the expert adviser is one which we could not even have conceived of posing a decade ago. Is unrestricted economic growth any longer a desirable objective? We should note that it is pointless to ask this question in a national context only. Not only are the national economies of developed countries dependent upon the exploitation of the resources, and often upon irremediable damage to the ecosystem, or other areas of the world, but it would be improper if not immoral, and impractical if not improper for the developed countries to call a halt to economic growth without considering the side-effects upon the economies of less fortunate nations. Even to prescribe that economic growth must halt or be severely restricted in the richer areas of the world alone will mean that growth in the poorer countries will be very much slower than would otherwise have been the case, and than equity if not prudence would suggest was desirable, and would be likely to tail off at a lower level. Nevertheless, unrestricted growth has equally unfortunate political side-effects, since the evidence even of the post-war era would suggest that it results in a widening rather than a closing of the gap between rich and poor areas of the world. It would seem to follow that restrictions on growth must therefore, if they are both to be effective and to avoid undesirable effects, be selective, in such a way as to encourage more rapid growth in the less developed countries, with the implication of some growth in defined economic areas of the richer nations, possibly with retrenchment elsewhere. This means on the one hand that there must be detailed and coherent international planning and agreement, and on the other that there must be a greater effort than heretofore to secure a redistribution of wealth and resources from the richer to the poorer nations. The international machinery for such action exists, but it has not hitherto been effective. It will not be so until statesmen of all countries and particularly of the developed countries can be convinced of the dangers which selfishness, obstinacy, and unrestricted competition with their neighbours can bring to all mankind and to their own nations in particular. If then "enlightened self-interest" is to be the slogan, it is up to the international community of experts to convince politicians and those whom they represent where their self-interest lies and to show them where enlightenment may be sought. The first duty here must therefore lie with such bodies as the Commonwealth Human Ecology Council rather than with politicians themselves.

Some immediate progress on the international level may be made by concentrating upon formulation of agreements to control and regulate carefully defined and specific activities. Such agreements may be negative in character, like that drafted by IMCO regulating the conditions for the transport by sea of oil in bulk. Such negative agreements can only be effective if their breach entails the imposition of penal sanctions. For this to happen, every nation must be a party to them, and there must be an effective system, and preferably a rapid system too, of dispensing international justice. The International Court has proved an admirable body, but its workings have been slower than might be thought desirable. In any event, too many issues, even when covered by international agreements, still come before national courts, which may in some countries dispense justice with an uneven hand. One lesson therefore is that in a world which is shrinking as rapidly as ours we must move just as rapidly towards the internationalisation of organs of justice. Equally, unless the verdict of such bodies is accepted by every nation, which means that the rest of the international community must be prepared to use at least economic sanctions to ensure that it is so accepted, then it is useless; if any tiny nation, even one without a coast-line, can provide a flag of convenience, and is prepared to disregard the verdict of the international community, and can do so with impunity, then there is little hope.

Historically, most international agreements in this field have been of the type I have just described. We may however look in the future towards a greater development of more positive agreements, designed to ration and control the use of natural resources on a world basis, or even

to further growth of those resources where they be living resources
rather than mineral. Again it is often pointless seeking to do this on a
national basis only, especially when it is remembered that we are now
developing not only the traditional methods of harvesting the sea, but
also looking, as would have been unimaginable until very recently, at the
exploitation of mineral resources hidden below the ocean floor. So far
the signs are not encouraging. In recent years each nation with a coast-
line has sought to expand both the limit of its territorial waters, and its
control over the continental shelf, if not other parts of the ocean bed.
The claim is already advanced that the continental slope is an integral
part of national territory. This fragmentation of control of the ocean
and ocean floor cannot be healthy. Unfortunately it is the largest and
most powerful nations of the world who are the worst sinners in this
respect. If any control is to be exercised over their activities, then one
must look to the smaller nations, and perhaps particularly to those with
no coast-line at all, to safeguard the interests of the world community
through the United Nations Organisation.

Even at a national level the problem is made worse by our ignorance
of the extent of our natural resources. When this problem is magnified
to an international scale, it would seem reasonable to assume that the
estimating error will be magnified along with it. It is hard to see how
even in Britain we can impose sensible controls on the exploitation of
resources below ground level until IGS has completed its geological
mapping of the British Isles and their off-shore waters. The problem on
both the national and the international scale is the same — inadequate
funding. It is absurd that there should be unemployed geologists in
Britain, and others who can find employment only by working for
commercially motivated enterprises abroad, when we are still so ignorant
of the extent of the resources we are consuming, and hence of the extent
to which the damage we are doing to the ecosystem is avoidable.

The same lesson may be learned from the history of the use of
chemical compounds which have ultimately proved to have a deleterious
effect, or an effect which is not yet fully and properly understood. A
good example is perhaps the use of organchloride pesticides, although
the story may be paralleled in a distinct though related sphere in the
administration of inadequately tested drugs directly to human beings.
Just as worrying is the administration of drugs, the effects of concentra-
tions of which upon man are not yet known, indirectly through their
use in animal husbandry. Comprehensive systems of national control,
with a total prohibition upon the administration of artificial products to
human beings, to animals, or to the land, until they have been exhaus-
tively tested and certified by a governmental rather than a commercial
agency, is here the first step towards sanity. While this is now widely
recognised, the machinery remains inadequate and fragmented; above all
the funding is again at too low a level. There are many ways in which

such work can be funded, and it is not my task to argue for one or the other to-day. Nevertheless it might seem reasonable that those who have most gained by the successful application of new artificial products should bear a substantial part of the cost of testing and certifying them. Even when this first step has been taken there is a long way to go. On the one hand, because of the danger of long term and unforeseen ecological effects, we must move towards continuous monitoring of the use of such products, and on the other we must seek international agreement, on a country-to-country basis, or on a world scale, to ensure compatibility of testing and certification procedures.

All of these are essentially political matters, since it is only the will of the community as a whole, its legislators and its administration, which can ensure that rapid progress is made. There are clear economic implications in what I have said already. There must be a shift of resources, however it is accomplished, from profit-motivated to socially orientated and socially controlled activities. This is no longer a question of political philosophy. I would argue that it ceased to be so when it was first realised that the control of epidemic disease depended upon an adequate system for maintaining adequate standards of public sanitation. Nevertheless, the emphasis has since moved steadily towards social control and orientation of an ever larger proportion of national and international resources. This argument cuts across many of the economic theories or nostrums advanced by political pundits: a return to a world where conditions of perfect free competition obtained, assuming that they ever did so obtain, is for example a recipe for ecological disaster, whatever might be the economic and social effects.

The second political lesson from what I have said hitherto is, surprisingly, in the field of foreign affairs. If we may assume, as I am sure we all hope that we may, that man is not going to destroy himself with a bang through an atomic holocaust, then it becomes ever more important that the emphasis of international negotiation should move away from its traditional concern with the balance of military power and the maintenance of political spheres of influence, towards ensuring that man does not destroy himself with a whimper through the destruction, accidentally and unwilled, of the ecosystem in which he lives. This means that there must be no diminution, but rather an increase, in diplomatic activity and in the resources devoted to it, but also that the type of diplomat we shall require in the future is likely to have rather different qualifications from some of those we have employed (and I shall not to-day say how, in my view, successfully or unsuccessfully we have employed them) in the past. We have entered the age of the scientifically qualified, or at least the scientifically understanding diplomat.

All of this has a further implication which lies in part at least in the political sphere. Our education system must be geared to give us the manpower we require for the tasks I have set out, in adequate numbers, and educated to a high enough level. This does not mean that all students in future must pursue a course in human ecology, however desirable that may seem to some of those, not least in the institution where we are gathered to-day, who have devoted themselves with much zeal to the provision of such courses. It does mean that an increasing proportion of the population must be educated to as a high a level as the nation can afford, and that most of them should receive as part of their total educational package some instruction in the basic principles of scientific reasoning and method, in the relationship of man to man in human society, and in the relationship of society as a whole to the environment in which it exists. I would in any event wish to argue that this was desirable on other grounds, both educational and social, but it now becomes a categorical imperative. At the same time we must ensure that adequate places are provided in higher education specifically for those who wish to study all or any of the many disciplines which relate to the interests of this Conference. I suppose it is safe for me, trained as a classicist and ancient historian, to say this, since at least I cannot be accused of bias towards my own discipline!

There is one further problem which has national and international implications to which I must allude to-day. I have left it to this point because it is more contentious and because it does not relate easily to what I have been saying so far. Every one of the tasks which we shall discuss at this Conference will become steadily more difficult unless there is some sharp diminution in the rate of growth of the population of the world. That applies just as much to the developed as to the under-developed countries. It is too easy to argue that the teeming Indians or Chinese are the source of the world's problems. In general it is not true. It is the teeming populations of the developed countries of the world, sometimes lower in absolute numbers than those of some countries in the third world, but almost always with a higher overall consumption of resources, those resources being drawn not only from the land area where the population lives, but from every corner of the globe. We should remember to-day that just over the hill, in south-east Lancashire and north-east Cheshire, is the most intensive concentration of population in Europe and hence in the world. Clearly any form of compulsory birth control, national or international, is impossible, on religious, political and humanitarian grounds. It does however seem to me to be imperative that governments make available the means of birth control to every adult person, with a subsidy from public funds at least where this is economically and socially necessary, and with adequate publicity, not to say propaganda, to ensure that the availability of these means is universally known and understood. Their use must remain a matter for individual choice. It does not however seem to me to be sensible to argue that because some object to the use of

methods of birth control, all or even some should be deprived of the
opportunity to use them if they so desire. To argue that the possibility
of every potential human life developing must be ensured by the
prohibition of birth control or by making access to the means of it as
difficult as possible, may become tantamount to arguing that all mankind or a substantial part of it shall perish in misery. That all should die
so that some may be created does not seem to me to be logical. I
recognise however that others may differ from me on this, on religious
or other grounds, and I respect their right so to do. If however what I
have said is generally acceptable, it follows that we have identified a
further need for qualified manpower in the provision of advice on birth
control.

At the national level, further problems remain. The first concerns
the machinery of government. The appointment of a Secretary of State
for the Environment is clearly a big step in the right direction, but
experience indicates that the existence of a single Minister at the head
of a Department does not guarantee a unity of view or approach within
it. Here however the signs are hopeful. The development of the use of
modern management techniques in government, the use of output
budgeting, the institution of PAR, should ensure that every governmental programme is subjected to the scrutiny of those concerned
with other programmes which may overlap, or duplicate it, and that
the planning of population distribution, of communication systems,
of housing provision, and of the preservation or use of natural
amenities and resources, should be interrelated and seen as a coherent
whole. As a back-stop we have, of course, the Cabinet, its team of
senior advisers, now supplemented by Lord Rothschild's group, and
the annual PESC exercises. At the same time a systems approach to
problems is gradually permeating government. Thus it is no longer
accepted as crudely as it might have been 10 years ago that cutting a
motorway like a swathe through the countryside will ease traffic
problems elsewhere and hence lessen the total damage to the environment; many would now argue that to do this and nothing else is merely
to move some problems of congestion from one place to another, and
probably to increase the total traffic flow, with the result that overall
damage to the environment has increased and not diminished. If
damage is to be minimised, all transportation systems, and each part of
each system, must be seen as forming an interlocking whole, the operation of which must be optimised both socially and ecologically, as well
as economically. There is however one central political problem which
remains unsolved in this field, and that is the degree to which central
government can rightly and properly coerce, albeit in an indirect fashion,
the individual. If environmental damage is to be minimised then it is
inescapable that the negative powers of central government shall be
great and shall be used.

At the same time, it is inescapable in a free enterprise or mixed economy that the positive powers of central government to initiate economic activity where it might not be profitable in strictly commercial terms so to do, shall also be great. There is a case for the simplification of controls, but no case for a bonfire of controls, if further continuous damage to the ecosystem is to be avoided. Already problems of urban sprawl generated in the post-war era *outside* the south-east of England are considerable. Increasing affluence produces a new order and scale of difficulty. It is now becoming unfortunately fashionable to purchase small areas of woodland as a country retreat, to fence them, to inhabit them at weekends — and to destroy them and everything that lives within them. Controls here are inadequate; perhaps we are always one danger behind in the imposition of controls, as the recent furore over the indiscriminate tipping of cyanide equally shows.

Positive measures to ensure not only the preservation but the development·of the natural environment are equally essential. We have come a long way since the early days of the Forestry Commission, with its unbounded enthusiasm for planting straight rows of conifers whether or not they were the natural or the most appropriate tree to the area. Even here however we must recognise that there is a difficult and imprecise boundary between the concept of preserving and developing for human benefit, and that of preserving and developing for human use. The affluent motor age means that all of us like to escape into, to use, and to enjoy the rural areas of our country. Unhappily we also destroy them. It is imperative therefore that it be recognised by the community and by its leaders that an amenity may be no less an amenity if it is not open to all who come. Maintaining an ecological balance may be of the greatest benefit of mankind, but it may be impossible if mankind insists on going in his thousands every weekend to see that it is being maintained, and literally digging up the roots to inspect them.

I end on a loud, but I hope not discordant note. All that I have said implies that politicians must ensure that resources are available to the scientific community for the investigation of the environment, for inquiry into the means of preserving and developing the ecosystem, and for giving the best advice that is available to those who must make political decisions. This cannot be done unless there are resources available at national level for the funding of research, and unless the decision as to the use of a substantial part of those funds is left to the scientific community or its representatives. The recent Rothschild recommendations fly in the face of this principle. When it is remembered that the working of many governmental research stations — broadly those for which the former Ministry of Technology was and the present Department of Trade and Industry is responsible — is in any event largely or wholly dictated by the requirements of government as they are identified by senior officials and politicians, and that a large part of our research effort goes into the maintenance of our Defence capability, it then becomes all the more imperative to ensure that the judgment of the scientific community as to priorities for research is not only respected but seen to be respected. This can only happen if that community itself allocates resources for a substantial number of projects. It follows clearly that the work of the NERC, of ARC, of MRC and of SRC should continue broadly in the way that it has done heretofore, without excessive direct interference by officials and Ministers. Equally, it follows that there must be real growth in the resources available to the Research Councils in the future, rather than the apparent growth and real decline which has been the pattern of the last few years.

Since this matter is under debate at this very moment, it is perhaps one of the most important tasks that we can set outselves to-day and tomorrow, that we should send out from this Conference a clear and unanimous view upon the Rothschild proposals.

Discussion

Dr. M. B. Halliday, Leicester Polytechnic. Since that was clearly a political speech, might I be permitted a political question? Could I ask Mr. Fowler what his government did when it was in power to ameliorate pollution caused by the nationalised industries over which it presumably had control?

G. T. Fowler. It was not a political speech, which is why I used the phrase "in recent years" when talking about the resources available to the research councils. My own government's record is no better than that of the present government either in that field or in the one to which you allude. There is a great deal of political education needing to be done, by, for example, those present here today. Otherwise you can't blame politicians if they act out of ignorance when the facts are not made available to them.

Professor M. J. L. Hussey, Open University. It is logically impossible to deny that *provided* the requisite action is taken, there will be no need to fear future environmental catastrophes. However, an awareness that particular actions *should* be taken does not necessarily imply that they *will* be taken. Is Mr. Fowler confident that politicians will, in fact, behave as he quite rightly says they must?

G. T. Fowler. On the national level the situation is much more hopeful than even a couple of years ago. There is a real growth of awareness among politicians of all parties. On the international level I don't think the situation is nearly as hopeful. Too many statesmen at the world level are pre-occupied with 19th century questions and do not seem to be aware that we may not even see the 21st century.

D. R. Hannay. I sympathise with your comments on the Rothschild Report, but if you require that politicians become more scientifically aware, then the degree of political direction of scientific effort will increase.

G. T. Fowler. Government does already control the majority of the research it finances. The research councils, controlled largely by scientists, represent a minority of government spending, but it is important that at least the principles underlying the allocation of that proportion of expenditure be understood by the politicians. What I am suggesting is that politicians should at least have the degree of competence in scientific matters to be able to appreciate, and if need be question, the advice proffered by the scientific community. I am not suggesting that ministers themselves should take the decisions, but it is advisable that they understand them.

3
Employment Prospects

B. GREGSON-ALLCOTT

1. Introduction

The name "Human Ecologist" used in the context of this symposium covers all the areas of the study of man in relation to his environment. When trying to determine the present and future pattern of employment of people who had been educated in this field it quickly became apparent that it was not worthwhile to try to distinguish human ecologist from ecologist. The present and future patterns of employment for ecologists are firmly based on the relationship between man and his environment. It is difficult therefore to distinguish a microbiologist working on pollution problems for a river authority from a conservation officer for a local authority in terms of this symposium's definition of a Human Ecologist. They both have a certain expertise and technical knowledge and their work has a direct bearing on the quality of the environment. Whether or not they are professional biologists is, however, another matter and this is a topic which will be discussed more fully in due course.

2. Background

Inevitably the background is educational and here a number of trends have been occurring at the same time. Some of these have been examined in the recent report on biological manpower[1]. There has been in the past few years, and there will continue to be, increasing numbers of biologists produced by the educational system. One has only to look at the range of courses which are available post A-level to see this. The working group came to the conclusion that the demand for biological jobs from graduates would exceed their supply in government service, in industry and even in teaching and this latter despite the paucity of graduate biology teachers in secondary schools. It is interesting to note in this context the experience of the Institute of Biology. Courses for MIBiol by examination have been running in technical colleges and the (now) polytechnics since 1964. The Ecology and Behaviour option was added in 1968 and this caters almost exclusively for teachers who wish to gain honours graduate status. To date some 50 students have taken the Part II examination and of these 41 have passed.

There is, however, the spectre of present and future graduate unemployment. This is not a simple problem with a simple answer and perhaps the term itself is a misnomer. Nevertheless the attitudes of graduates to the nature of the job they will seek on first employment are changing. We will see, in the future, graduates not only in different levels of employment but also in different areas of employment.

Alongside this is the realisation that perhaps a specialist biological education at first degree level may not be always appropriate for some areas of employment. It may be more appropriate to leave some specialist training to after the first degree. At present most postgraduate training of biologists is carried out in traditional biological areas of study. However, other areas might be appropriate and, as will be indicated, they are already being considered by students and employers.

Ecology teaching is being placed on a firm quantitative basis. It is no longer simply a descriptive science and many of the changes in ecology teaching have been pioneered in technical colleges and polytechnics. The Higher National Certificate and Diploma in Applied Biology have a core of quantitative biology from which develops specialist areas of study. Many of the micro-biology courses, running in some twenty colleges, are concerned with aspects of pollution particularly water pollution and four colleges run applied ecology or pollution studies options. Some CNAA degrees — notably that of Hatfield Polytechnic — develop ecological training from a firm quantitative basis and this has been basic philosophy since the course was introduced in 1966. New university courses include Human Ecology at the New University of Ulster and Environmental Sciences at East Anglia. The changes, however, are not confined to higher education and the Schools Council Project Environment and the proposed A-level in Environmental studies are interesting developments.

3.   Employment

The changes in the structure of courses and in the attitudes of students to their courses will inevitably mean that there will be people who are not satisfied with the traditional role of the ecologist. In an investigation of the possible areas of employment there seemed to be a reasonable split into two groups of people.

Firstly those whose biological education leads them to want to work as a biologist in the applied field. These are people whose biology is useful to them in the employment sense and meaningful in the professional sense, i.e. they can obtain MIBiol after suitable experience.

Secondly there are those whose biological education gives them a broad background to the biological problems of society and who want to work in areas outside those of applied biology. In order to become qualified these people have to pursue other courses and become members of other professional bodies. They are therefore people whose biology is useful but not meaningful in a professional sense.

4. Present Position

What is the present position regarding employment of ecologists and what are the attitudes of students to their courses? The information available is very limited but the following tables give a useful guide provided the widest definition of ecologist is exercised.

Table I. Posts obtained by MIBiol students in Entomology and Plant Pathology, Wolverhampton Polytechnic, 1967-71

Posts obtained	Numbers of Students	
	Entomology	Plant Pathology
AEO/EO in Nature Conservancy, Agricultural Research Council.	2	5
EO in University Departments and Research Assistants.	1	3
Studying for higher degrees — MSc/MPhil/PhD	4	6
Teaching/lecturing	2	3
Other biological posts	3	1
Non-biological posts	1	1
Students (from those qualifying in June 1971) still seeking relevant employment.	2	1

Reproduced by kind permission of G. Ayerst and A. M. Gower.

Table II. First Employment of those who graduated from Hatfield Polytechnic — Applied Biology in 1970.

Posts obtained	Numbers of students
Research studentships	10
Other degrees/courses	4
Teaching/teacher training	3
Industry (research)	6
Industry (non-research)	6
Hospital/medical	4
Technicians	4
Accountancy	1
Technical adviser	1
Unemployed	1
Not known	2

Reproduced by kind permission of K. W. Thomas.

Of those graduating from Hatfield a number of the posts obtained were in fields related to ecology. Two of the industrial research posts were at Rothamsted Experimental Station, the technical adviser's job was in plant protection and one of the technician jobs was in public health. It is claimed in some quarters that there is a need for graduates in agriculture, horticulture and related areas of work and Tables I and II show that recent graduates or their equivalents are obtaining posts in these areas. The report of the Nottingham Appointments Board[2] also indicates that agricultural science graduates find jobs, not surprisingly, in agriculture; six out of a total of thirty-nine who went into employment. A further thirteen entered government service or the armed forces and eighteen entered industry and commerce. Perhaps a number of these will have taken jobs related to their degree. Only one agricultural science graduate was unemployed six months after graduating.

Another group of students who have specialised in ecology but at a lower level than that of a degree are those who followed the Applied Ecology option of an HND in Applied Biology. The following students from Brighton Technical College took this option together with, in most cases, micro-biology.

Table III. Posts obtained by students of the Applied Ecology option of an HND in Applied Biology from Brighton Technical College.

Posts obtained	Numbers of students
Horticulture research	2
Fisheries/marine laboratories	4
Water Board	3
River Authority	1
Toxicology/nematology	2
University technicians (nitrogen fixation unit)	3
Veterinary surveys	1
Antarctic survey	1
Forensic science	1

Reproduced by kind permission of Dr. U. K. Smith.

Their present pattern of employment ranges from toxicology to river authority work and it is interesting to note that one of these students applied for a job with the Nature Conservancy only to find some four hundred other applicants.

The employment of graduates in Government services and in the water resources industries are shown in Tables IV and V.

Table IV. Biologists in Government Service 1970[3].

Organisation	Number of Posts in Biology and ecology
ARC	102
Pest control laboratories	24
Freshwater Fisheries laboratories	13
Anti-locust	33
NERC	94
Forestry Commission	6

Table V. Biologists employed in organisations concerned with Water Resources 1970[4].

Organisation	Number of posts
Government	116
Public Industry	25
Industrial Research Organisations	4
Private Industry	16
River Authorities (29)	40
Water Undertakings (228)	44
Sewage Undertakings	12
(1,400 authorities with 5,000 works)	

The overall position is also shown in the Report of the Working Group on Biological Manpower[1] which indicates that a total of 2,744 biologists employed by the Government and Research Councils, 195 were ecologists and of the total of 1,711 biologists employed by industrial research, twelve were ecologists.

However the overall figures giving the present employment of biologists and ecologists have to be treated with caution since they do not indicate the number of posts which will become available in any one year. It is the turnover of jobs that is important when we try to predict the future pattern of employment of ecologists. The Government employs nearly 3,000 biologists but the total number of new posts available for graduates in 1972 will be of the order of 130; i.e. just over 4% of the total. Taking the Working Group's figures this means that the Government may employ about ten ecologists during 1972. Even if this figure were doubled or trebled it is still insignificant compared with the total number of ecologists produced.

5.   Attitudes of students

What are the attitudes of students to their courses in respect of their future employment prospects? Many do not realise that they will be holding administrative or managerial posts perhaps shortly after graduating. The Survey of Professional Scientists[5] gives details of scientists in managerial posts. At age 25 and below 16.8% held such posts but this percentage increases rapidly to 43.4% at age 30-34 and reaches a figure of over 70% at age 45 and over. It is a matter of conjecture whether biologists are fairly or unfairly treated in such a survey. Nevertheless it must be true to say that biologists will follow this general upward trend and will increasingly find themselves in managerial and administrative positions. This surely is no bad thing because biologists have a positive contribution to make to administration by virtue of their biological training which deals with complex interrelating themes.

A survey conducted among those students who had completed the MSc course in Conservation at University College, London during the first nine years of its existence (1960-69) indicated that 71% thought the course was useful as vocational training for a job in conservation, applied ecology or planning. 44% of the students indicated that it was also useful as a change of discipline although from what is not known. A small number of students indicated a further change of direction in that they followed this course with a Diploma in Town Planning (2) an MSc in Geography (1) and an Institute of Landscape Architects qualification (1). The nature of their present work was also interesting.

Table IV. Present employment of students who have completed the MSc in Conservation from University College, London.

PhD in a university of college of advanced technology	11
Nature Conservancy	8
Other conservation work (Naturalists Trusts)	4
Countryside Commission	3
Planning (other than above)	5
Ecological research	5
Housewife	6
Lecturing	4
School teaching	3
Forestry	2
Agricultural Research (Rothamsted)	1

The categories above were selected from the replies. Although eight of the respondents are doing a PhD full-time, several others are registered externally or have already completed a thesis. Table reproduced by kind permission of Dr. F. B. O'Connor.

Although these results are by no means more than a preliminary

screening of the fifty-two replies to the survey, they do indicate in some measure that students are looking beyond the traditional role of specialised ecologist and it is important to realise this when planning courses.

6. Attitudes of Employers

The attitude of employers is more difficult to assess. Many industrial establishments would be willing to consider ecology graduates for employment in areas such as personnel, industrial training or marketing. It may be that they could replace the arts graduate in these fields. However there is no evidence to show that employers will do this.

Many people are of the opinion that ecologists will be useful in planning and conservation departments of local authorities. Some authorities have already appointed biologists to such departments, e.g. Cheshire and Devon, but at the moment they are few and far between. A number of Authorities have one officer who has general conservation responsibilities but these are generally not ecologists. Indeed there are some positive indications that ecologists are not wanted.

It has not been possible to conduct an exhaustive survey and conclusions are necessarily subjective. However, there has been no indication that there is both a need and a requirement for ecologists. It would seem that society in general and educators in particular feel that there is a need for ecologists. Specialist ecologists will be needed for teaching and research in polytechnics and universities but perhaps more particularly there is a need in school teaching. Our concern for the future of our environment must be passed on to pupils before they leave school. Perhaps this may be one of many interrelated themes which could be developed during the extra year at school when the leaving age is raised. We must remember that 50% of the pupils leave at the age of fifteen.

There is no real evidence that there is a demand from industry for ecologists. Ought we to be asking the question "Are we producing too many specialist ecologists now?". I have seen no evidence to suggest that more specialist ecologists ought to be produced. The University Grants Committee[6] figures for 1969-70 do not put ecologists into a separate group but there is no evidence that they will not suffer the same fate as the biologist (9.9% unemployed six months after graduating), the botanist (8.2%), or zoologist (9.9%). In this context the agriculture or forestry graduate emerges only slightly better (7.7%). It is also interesting to note that the Social, Administrative and Business Studies Group, and in the Architecture and Town Planning Group, 6.6% and 10.0% respectively are unemployed.

7. What of the future?

Many river authorities employ biologists at graduate and technician level for ecological and other jobs. The Avon and Dorset River Authority has three graduate biologists and will be employing a further graduate and non-biological graduate assistant. This sort of pattern is repeated in other Authorities and the future will show a continued growth in this area. It is unusual to hear a Government report called "exciting" but this was the term used by one person when describing the recent circular from the Department of the Environment . Certainly it is far-reaching. The provision of ten all-purpose authorities will create a career structure within the area of environmental control which will enable a person with the right academic and personal qualities to move into an administrative capacity which, at its highest point, will surely be equivalent to a top Civil Service appointment. Biologists and ecologists could play an important part in this structure. Over the last five to ten years the river authorities and water boards have used biologists in roles which were traditionally those of the chemist or engineer. The increasing employment of biologists at the lower levels will create a pyramid structure which may enable a biologist to be considered for top appointments alongside chemists and engineers.

It will be important however for the biologist or ecologist to learn another trade and here the original classification must be returned to. The second group were those whose biological education was useful but not professionally meaningful. The Royal Town Planning Institute, the Institute of Water Pollution Control, the Institute of Landscape Architects and the Association of Public Health Inspectors are all examples of professional institutes who could accept an ecologist only if he were prepared to follow a course leading either to their examinations or to a recognised exemption from them.

Contacts with a number of people from universities, professional institutes and local authorities have convinced me that a specialist ecologist is unemployable in the fields of town planning, water resources, urban conservation, landscape architecture, etc., unless he has a second qualification related to the technology of one of these fields. Indeed the present attitude seems to be that when there are sufficient applicants with an initial training in a discipline related to the job, they would be considered in preference to those who had an ecological training and who wished to start or were part of the way through a second training.

This does not seem to give much hope for the employment prospects of the ecologist unless he can readily get a qualification of professional status. If he gets the second qualification he may be too old for the job and if he doesn't get it, he may not be offered the job in the first place. In this context it is interesting to note the efforts being made by some institutions of higher education. The proposed CNAA degree in Environmental Studies at Thames Polytechnic is an interdisciplinary degree run by the Biology Department and involving studies in civil engineering, architecture, sociology, economics and law. It is intended that graduates may either go into industry or become immediately qualified as Public Health Inspectors by exemption from the professional examination. The degree in Environmental Health from Aston University which is run by the Department of Building also leads to the

Final Diploma of the Public Health Inspectors Education Board and
'A' level Biology is acceptable as one of the entrance qualifications.
Another is the Stirling degree in Technological Economics where a
major course in economics is linked with a major course in a science
which may be biology.

8. Conclusions

The crystal ball for the employment of ecologists is particularly hazy,
Perhaps even more so than for the other areas of biology. There is very
little evidence, and conclusions drawn from such evidence that there is
must be subjective and extremely tentative. Nevertheless the one conclusion which seems to emerge from discussions with very many people
with different backgrounds and expertise over the whole field of
ecology, is that if the ecologist is to be employed in fields such as town
planning or urban conservation, he must have a training which is tech-
nologically competent and professionally recognisable. We think as
biologists that an ecological background will enable a person to make a
positive contribution in these fields. It would seem that we have yet to
convince the employers of such people of the validity of our claim.

References

1   *Report of the Working Group on Biological Manpower*, Cmnd
     4737, HMSO, 1971.
2   *Careers and Appointments Board Annual Report 1970*, University
     of Nottingham.
3   *Biologist 1970*, 17(5), 200.
4   *Biologist 1971*, 18(2), 60.
5   *The Survey of Professional Scientists 1968*, Ministry of Tech-
     nology, HMSO, 1970.
6   *First Employment of University Graduates 1969-70*, University
     Grants Committee, HMSO, 1971.
7   Reorganisation of Water and Sewage Services: Government
     Proposals and Arrangements for Consultation, Circular 92/71,
     Department of the Environment, HMSO, 1971.

Discussion

P. Carter. I am concerned that we concentrate too much on vocational
training. There is also a responsibility to the community at large
to encourage education in human ecology, not only because that
study is essential for the community, but also because of the intellectual
rewards arising from a broad study of the human environment.

B. Gregson-Allcott. Unfortunately, intending students are already
being put off the study of certain subjects because they realise the lack

of employment prospects in those subjects. We do have a responsibility to inform prospective students of their future employment prospects. *P. Carter.* I think we can be more optimistic about future employment prospects. Students starting courses in the near future will be looking for jobs in three or four years time. By then, employment prospects in the field of human environment studies are likely to have increased considerably.

H. Roper. With regard to planning studies, I would not be so pessimistic about employment prospects for graduates with an ecological training. Planners are increasingly recognising the need for ecologists and this recognition will, in time, be translated into improved employment prospects for those who are ecologically orientated. I recently asked a group of our own students what they thought was the most important subject missing from their course and they all agreed it was ecology.

B. Gregson-Allcott. While I hope your predictions are correct, we have to remember that at the present time the situation is not so promising.

Professor P. J. Newbould, New University of Ulster. Concerning the employment of ecologically orientated staff in planning offices I should mention that the British Ecological Society and the Royal Town Planning Institute are hoping to arrange a conference on the place of ecologists in planning. This should be held early in 1973.

Professor H. Bowen-Jones, Durham University. A major future problem will be educating prospective employers in the need for human ecologists, a "man-description" rather than a "job-description" problem.

Part 2
Contributions of the Principal Disciplines

4

The Contribution of Ecology to the Study of Human Ecology

P. J. NEWBOULD

1. Introduction

The ecology content of a Human Ecology course is like the history content of a European History course; the whole course is ecological. A few years ago ecologists were, in general, only interested in natural plant and animal communities, unsullied by human activity, and human ecology, especially in the U.S.A., tended to be a branch of sociology. However, Bews (1935) and later Fraser Darling (1951, 1955) developed a broader concept of human ecology.

Ecology has now provided a conceptual framework within which human ecology, the ecology of human populations and factors affecting their survival may be studied. I will list some features of this conceptual framework and then try to elucidate them and their application to human ecology by examples.

(i)   The ecosystem concept including the taxonomic, structural and functional organisation of the ecosystem.

(ii)   The functional model of the ecosystem, involving energy flow and mineral cycling.

(iii)   The concept of up to five sets of potentially independent factors controlling the ecosystem.

(iv)   The dynamic nature of ecosystems; their tendency to develop from simple, uniform, productive, unstable systems to complex, stable, diverse, protective systems.

(v)   The continuity of ecosystems assured by the transmission of energy patterns, genetic information and, in the case of human ecosystems, cultural information through time.

The application of these concepts to human society is outlined in a remarkable new book by H. T. Odum, *Environment, Power and Society.* This covers so much so summarily that its full evaluation will take several years.

2.   The Ecosystem

The ecosystem, a term adopted by Tansley (1935), is an organised assemblage of plants and animals with their immediate environment

37

(especially soil and micro-climate). The scale of an ecosystem being studied is defined by its student. It may be a fallen tree-trunk, a ten acre stand of woodland, the forest of the Amazon basin or, indeed the whole biosphere.

The taxonomic organisation of an ecosystem refers to the number and abundance of plant and animal species comprising it. The Wytham Wood ecosystem which has been intensively studied by Elton and his colleagues has already been shown to include more than 2,000 different species of animal and more will yet be discovered. Tropical rain forest may be the most species rich ecosystem in the world. In an intensive study of an area in Malaya, Poore (1964) records in an area of 105 hectares, 2629 large trees belonging to 381 species. The structural organisation refers to vertical and horizontal pattern, the characteristic layering of the forest and also its roots as well as the clumping together of individuals of the same species, often because young animals or plants are clustered around their parent or for reasons of environmental heterogeneity. The dominant plants impose structural pattern within which subsidiary plants and most of the animals find appropriate ecological niches. The accumulation of organic matter, whether in the soil or the standing crop is one aspect of structure.

Functional organisation is a theme originating from the work of Lindeman (1942) and greatly extended by Odum and others. It involves the concept of the ecosystem as a working system in which an input of energy counteracts entropy. The input derives from solar radiation fixed by plants in photosynthesis. Energy is dissipated by the respiration of all the organisms in the ecosystem. Mineral matter, unlike energy is not dissipated but cycled in the ecosystem.

3.   Energy flow and mineral cycling in ecosystems

The functioning of ecosystems is frequently described in terms of the transfer of energy and matter through trophic levels, such as primary producers, herbivores, carnivores, top carnivores, decomposers. These levels in the simplest case, represent a food chain; more usually this is a food network. Man himself, like many other animals, is an omnivore and overlaps several compartments. Energy flow in ecosystems as all other energy systems obeys the laws of thermodynamics, namely that energy may be transformed from one form to another but is neither created nor destroyed and that processes involving energy transformations will not occur spontaneously unless there is a degradation of energy from a non-random to a random form (Phillipson 1966).

To study the functioning of an ecosystem, which is an open system, the inputs and outputs of energy and matter must be measured. In some situations, such as many of the I.B.P. ecosystem studies the inputs and outputs are predominantly natural e.g. solar radiation, rainfall, rock weathering, drainage losses. Once these are identified and measured, attention can be focussed on processes internal to the ecosystem. In human ecosystems man may introduce larger energy inputs mostly derived from fossil fuel.

4.   Ecological factors

The composition structure and functioning of an ecosystem may be controlled by at least five sets of ecological factors capable of varying at least partly independently of one another. This is at once the strength and the difficulty of ecology. Precise predictions concerning changes in the elements and states of a system with five independent variables are not possible. But ecologists accustomed to attempting intuitive solutions to these complex multivariate systems, have devised possible approaches. One formulation of ecological factors is that used by Jenny (1941) to describe soil forming factors. He described soil as the resultant of climate, organisms, relief (= topography), parent material (of the soil) and time. This approach was subsequently taken up by Major (1951) who applied the same approach to ecosystems. It may be expressed as:

$$e = f (cl, o, r, p, t, \ldots).$$

The organisms present in an ecosystem are largely determined by the other factors; organisms as an independent variable refers to those species potentially available to an area, the regional fauna and flora. Technological man with his armoury of machinery, energy and chemicals may best be regarded as another independent variable. For purposes of study, four of the groups of factors are held as constant as possible but the fifth is caused to vary as much as possible, e.g. Perring's (1960) work on chalk grassland where he used both topography and climate as variables in different instances. Time as an independent variable implies change in ecosystems. It is often possible to specify T_0, a starting point for the ecosystem process under study, e.g. the time when farm land is abandoned may be T_0 for the change to forest vegetation.

5.   Change in ecosystems

Time is clearly rather different from the other factors mentioned. Many ecologists have studied change in ecosystems from the small scale "pattern and process" of Watt (1947) to the effect of major climatic changes revealed by various palaeoecological techniques such as pollen analysis. Most attention has been given to the way in which ecosystems come to progressively greater equilibrium with the environment, this being known as succession. It was the occasion of a grand debate in the thirties between Clements and Phillips, who erected a somewhat rigorous framework and Tansley (1935) who was more flexible in his approach. For present purposes I shall accept the general viewpoint of Odum (1969). He defines ecological succession in terms of three parameters.

(i)   It is an orderly process of community development that is reasonably directional and, therefore, predictable.

(ii)   It results from modification of the physical environment by the community; that is, succession is community-controlled even though the physical environment determines the pattern, the rate of change and often sets limits as to how far development can go.

(iii)   It culminates in a stabilised ecosystem in which maximum biomass (or high information content) and symbiotic functions between organisms are maintained per unit of available energy flow. In a word the "strategy" of succession as a short-term process is basically the same as the "strategy" of long-term evolutionary development of the biosphere — namely, increased control of, or homeostasis with, the physical environment in the sense of achieving maximum protection from its perturbations.

Odum further illustrates the partitioning of total or gross photosynthesis between

(i)   accumulation of organic matter plus living biomass and

(ii)   maintenance, which is essentially community respiration.

As biomass increases, so maintenance costs increase. In the final stable climax ecosystem all the energy input goes in maintenance and there is no further accumulation of biomass. In the earlier developmental stages the energy destined for accumulation is equally available for harvest as a crop and its removal in this way will arrest further development without endangering the maintenance of biomass already accumulated. There is, in fact, a conflict between production and protection and a stable and productive landscape must include components of both. There is a compelling analogy between the development of an ecosystem towards its stable 100% maintenance situation and the growth of a new town where recurrent maintenance expenditure must eventually overtake capital investment in new works.

6.   The continuity of ecosystems
The accumulation of organic matter and living biomass gives continuity to successive ecosystems just as the accumulation of roads and buildings gives continuity to human systems. The taxonomic composition of an ecosystem at T_2 is dependent on its composition at T_1 plus local immigration or extinction during the period T_1 to T_2. Hence there is a considerable element of genetic continuity. In man-dominated ecosystems, man transmits culture, that is information, through time and this is a third element of continuity. One example of transmitted information not obviously accompanied by either genetic material or energy patterns is religion.

7.   Man in the ecosystem
These concepts are summarised in the ecosystem model in Fig. 1 although the dynamic nature of the ecosystem through time is not shown. Man is both a component of the ecosystem and a powerful ecological factor modifying it, by energy and mineral inputs and losses

(e.g. fertilisers, crops, machinery). Hunting and food-gathering man is solely a component of the ecosystem. So, generally, is subsistence agriculture man. Twentieth century man on the other hand is altering natural ecosystems faster, more fundamentally and over more of the world's surface than any other ecological factor. This model or some modification of it, seems to me a tolerable starting point for the description and comparison of the ecology of human communities. Some ecological properties of human populations are summarised in Table 1.

8. Levels of human organisation

(a) Food gatherers. Food gatherers are exemplified by the 'Kung Bushmen described by Lees (1969). Climate has a dominant role. The level of primary production is low, related to low rainfall (Walter 1964). The Bushmen feed selectively on what is produced and have regulatory customs (infanticide, system of sexual choice, etc.) which keeps their numbers within what the environment can support (25 to 40 per 100 sq. miles). Lee discusses the subsistence effort, S, necessary to sustain a group of Bushmen, which he quantifies as W/C where W is the number of man days of work and C is the number of man days of consumption. This is a form of ecological efficiency. For most non-human primates $S = 1/1$, and this in a sense represents the evolutionary starting point for man. The 'Kung Bushmen have values of S varying from 0.11 to 0.31 and an average diet of 2140 calories/person/day, although the calculated subsistence requirement for these rather small people is 1975 cal/person/day. This provides the basis for a simple energy flow diagram.

(b) Subsistence agriculture. Masefield (1970) has examined the carrying capacity of different types of land used for subsistence agriculture. In Buganda the land will support about 350 people per square mile and above that level, soil exhaustion, erosion and dietary deficiency ensue. Other areas of more or less humid tropics may have figures up to a thousand per square mile or in some rural areas of East Pakistan 2500 per square mile. In the dry tropics 200 to 500 is a more normal range. Masefield finds in East Africa that ungulate populations of 85,000 lb./sq. mile are supported and this would be equivalent to about 1,100 people. Since the level generally supported is below this, the ungulate seem to be more ecologically efficient than the men. Both men and ungulates frequently migrate both diurnally and seasonally and in general low density use frequently involves movement, whether it is the Bushmen gathering food, the migration of the great herds of game, movement around hunting grounds or shifting cultivation (see Butt 1970).

(c) More complex situations. A fair proportion of existing human ecological studies deal with island populations, other small isolated populations or primitive tribes, either hunting/food gathering, or some form of subsistence agriculture as listed above. It is relatively easy to apply ecological concepts in these situations. Man has now invented systems in which the greater part of the energy input derives from the use of fossil fuel. An intensive farm uses manufactured products including fertilisers, pesticides, concrete, wire, farm machinery, tractor fuel; in energy terms these may outweigh the food actually produced. Kneese *et al* (1970) have shown what happens to the photosynthesis in the U.S.A. (Table 2). The human population of the U.S.A. has fuel energy inputs several times greater than its food or wood inputs. Similarly agricultural systems, e.g. in Britain or Japan, are based on fossil fuel energy inputs of about the same magnitude as the crop yields. It would be useful to calculate some ratio of self sufficiency in which non-sustainable inputs such as minerals and fossil fuels or indeed imported food, are compared with the sustainable production of food and wood. If we heed the warning of Blueprint for Survival (*The Ecologist,* January 1972) societies should be deliberately moving towards greater sustainable self-sufficiency. The hundred-fold or more difference per caput energy availability between the U.S.A. and, for example, India or Pakistan, creates enormous problems of control and administration. The energy costs of the distribution of energy, including manufactured products are very high. Great modification of environment, some of it in the form of pollution, is inevitable.

High energy inputs allow the establishment of very high density human populations (1-2 x 10^5 per square mile in the more densely populated parts of London, New York or Calcutta) sustained by large extraneous inputs. High density, high mobility and high energy use create new forms of isolation — isolation by income group, by race and the isolation implicit in the rate of change of society, the so-called generation gap. Each form of isolation is partial, not total nor do they coincide. As man becomes an increasingly urban species, these forms of isolation supersede geographical isolation. Human populations become physically mixed but remain socially isolated.

This new situation, high density, high energy input, populations, spatially clustered and socially isolated is proving difficult to study, either by ecological or sociological methods. Crude social statistics based on sample surveys are difficult to handle because of the difficulty of isolating the human population being studied. Human society is changing faster than ever before. Terms like social disintegration are current but highly imprecise and emotive. Here is a major challenge to human ecology to develop a conceptual framework for studying this situation.

9.   Biosphere energetics
Deevey (1971) has summarized biosphere energetics, using a new unit, the geocalorie. I set out his findings in Table 3. The real difference

between energy flow in the biosphere now and two hundred years ago is in the 25 units of thermal energy used to maintain our present complex social and economic organisation. This is the component the ecologist finds it difficult to fit into his model. Since photosynthesis is only about 0.1% of solar radiation received, the fossil fuel thermal energy is no more than 0.008% of the radiation balance of the earth and presumably insignificant.

But the global human ecosystem with its 25 units of thermal energy differs in three important ways from the natural biosphere energy model. Firstly the thermal energy is much less evenly dispersed than the photosynthetic energy; its intensity in large cities is relatively enormous. Secondly the human ecosystem is much less stable, and therefore less predictable than the natural one. A competent and well-equipped ecologist visiting the planet 10,000 years ago would have had little difficulty in making ecological predictions valid for some hundreds of years, whereas now none of us can see at all clearly to the end of the century. And thirdly the thermal energy is almost certainly non-renewable.

10. Conclusion

Ecological concepts can be helpfully applied to simple situations, including islands, isolated communities, primitive tribes and subsistence agriculture communities. There remain problems in applying them to twentieth century urban man because the populations to be studied cannot be isolated and because inflows of energy and information tend to be very large compared to ecosystem energy flow deriving from solar radiation.

However, on a whole world or biosphere scale, as outlined above, ecological concepts are more easily applied since the limits of the system are definable and for most purposes it is a closed system (Spaceship Earth). Ecological concepts so applied by Forrester (1970) are currently leading to predictions of impending doom (Blueprint for Survival 1972) unless man quickly adopts ecological principles and an ecological life style.

11. References

Bews, J. W. (1935) *Human Ecology*, OUP, London.

Butt, A. J. (1970) Land use and social organisation of tropical forest peoples of the Guianas, in Garlick, J. P. & Keay, R. W. J. (eds.), *Human Ecology in the Tropics*, 33-50, Pergamon, Oxford.

Deevey, E. S. (1971) The chemistry of wealth, *Bulletin of the Ecological Society of America*, 52 (4), 3-8.

Ecologist (1972) Blueprint for Survival, *The Ecologist* 2(1), January 1972.

Forrester, J. W. (1970) *World Dynamics*, Wright Allen Press, Cambridge, Mass.

44 The Education of Human Ecologists

Fraser Darling, F. (1951) The ecological approach to the social sciences, *American Scientist* 39, 244- 56.

Fraser Darling, F. (ed.) (1955) *West Highland Survey,* OUP, London.

Jenny, H. (1941) *Factors of soil formation,* McGraw-Hill, New York.

Kneese, A. V., Ayres, R. U. & D'Arge, R. C. (1970) *Economics and the environment,* Resources for the Future, Washington.

Lee, R. B. (1969) 'Kung bushman subsistence: an input-output analysis, in Vayda, A. P. (ed.), *Environment and Cultural Behaviour,* 47-79, American Museum Sourcebooks in Anthropology, New York.

Lindeman, R. L. (1942) The trophic-dynamic aspects of ecology, *Ecology* 23, 399-418.

Major, J. (1951) A functional factorial approach to plant ecology, *Ecology* 32, 392-412.

Masefield, G. B. (1970) Food resources and production, in Garlick and Keay (see Butt above 59-66).

Odum, E. P. (1960) The strategy of ecosystem development, *Science* 164, 262-70, New York.

Odum, H. T. (1971) *Environment, Power and Society,* John Wiley, New York.

Perring, F. (1960) Climatic gradients of chalk grassland, *J. Ecol.* 48, 415-42.

Phillipson, J. (1966) *Ecological energetics,* Arnold, London.

Poore, M. E. D. (1964) Integration in the plant community, *J. Ecol.* 52, Supplement 213-26.

Tansley, A. G. (1935) The use and abuse of vegetational terms and concepts, *Ecology* 16, 284-307.

Walter, H. (1964) The role of ecology in the development of tropical and subtropical regions, *Proc. Tenth Int. Bot. Cong. Edinburgh,* 69-80.

Watt, A. S. (1947) Pattern and process in the plant community, *J. Ecol.* 35, 1-22.

Table 1

	Density, people/sq. mile of land.	Subsistence effort "farmers" or food-gathering days whole population or consuming days	Self-sufficiency ratio food energy extraneous energy
Non-human primates	—	1	no extraneous energy
'Kung Bushmen	0.25 – 0.4	0.11 – 0.31	no extraneous energy
Subsistence agriculture	200 – 500	0.1 – 0.3	1 : 1
India	320	—	—
Britain	460	0.03	c.1 : 20
U. S. A.	55	0.01	c.1 : 32
World	25	—	c.1 : 12
Densely populated city, London, N.Y.	160,000	all food imported into city	? 1 : 100

Table 2   *(Data from Kneese et al. 1970)*

U.S.A.	Dry weight 10^6 tons		
Net crops, harvested	59.3	available as food	32
Animal products	"	"	17.2
Fish	"	"	0.8
Total food			50.0
Fuel used			1448
Wood pulp and timber used			166 (10 recycled)

Thus $\dfrac{\text{food}}{\text{fuel and wood}}$ for U.S.A. $= \dfrac{1}{32}$

Table 3   *(Data from Deevey 1971)*

Biosphere photosynthesis	177	geocalories/year
World production/consumption of thermal energy, 1980	14.8	" "
World output of calories (respiration and growth) by domestic livestock	1.17	" "
World consumption of food by man (respiration and growth)	0.58	

1 geocalorie = 5.2×10^{18} calories = 1 calorie/cm^2 of earth's surface.

Ratio	Photosynthesis :	industry :	husbandry :	people
	300	25	2	1
	renewable	presumably non renewable	renewable	renewable

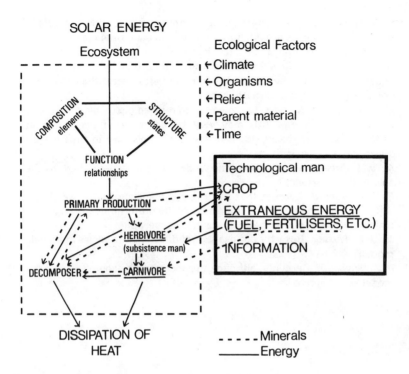

Discussion

M. J. L. Hussey. There appears to be a distinction between the approaches of the natural scientist and the technologist to human ecology, with the former requiring greater predictive precision from a model. Current criticisms of environmental models stem from their being considered from a scientific rather than a technological point of view. A good reason for constructing models is to find not precisely what will happen but what cannot be expected to happen. Putting bounds on possibilities seems to me to be important, and for that it is less than essential to get accurately detailed predictions.

E. Paget. Would it be too much of a generalisation to say that the parts of the world with the greatest amount of replaceable energy are the less developed countries?

P. J. Newbould. I would tend to agree here, particularly with regard to available solar energy, although utilisation of this energy will be dependant on many ecological factors and will include problems peculiar to precisely those areas with a high potential.

E. B. Worthington. A further point of interest is that while potentially useable solar radiation tends to be greatest in equatorial regions, this is true only for terrestrial ecosystems. For marine ecosystems this does not seem to be the case since the areas of minimum productivity are near the equator with much higher levels of productivity nearer the poles, this being largely related to nutrient supply.

P. J. Newbould. We have to remember that when discussing potentially available solar energy, this may vary by an order of magnitude in different parts of the world, whereas fossil fuels vary in their use by several orders of magnitude.

M. J. L. Hussey. Why is there this tendency to use energy flow as the sole form of currency?

P. J. Newbould. I accept that there is this tendency, but if we all use different currencies when building models, then this limits the degree to which our model-building efforts are interconvertible.

M. J. L. Hussey. But why not use several different currencies in a single model?

P. J. Newbould. Certainly, although this increases the complexity of the model building required.

5

The Role of Economics in the Study of the Human Environment

G. A. PETCH

The human environment is to a very large extent the product of the human beings themselves. They have made extensive changes in the natural physical environment: they have moved, if not mountains, at least not inconsiderable hills, they have replaced water with solid land; they have rendered extinct more than one living organism. Further, they have imposed such physical modifications on the landscape as roads, fields,. mines, factories, villages and towns; they have introduced large elements of organization into the environment by a complex of institutions such as countries, parliaments, joint stock companies and trade unions. Their "atmospheric" contributions to their own environment include not only pollution and noise, but the degree of equity and personal freedom which exist and the stress and strain of a society which offers all of us the lure of financial gain, greater status, and greater possibilities of self-expression, as well as the fear of unemployment, poverty and descent in the social scale.

Human ecology is therefore perforce a social study in a way which plant and animal ecology are not. There are additional reasons why this should be true. The earthworm perseveres with the formation of vegetable mould no matter whether it is working in a capitalist or communist society; nor does he take time off from the vegetable mould to bewail his unhappy lot. The human equivalent of the earthworm is not so indifferent. These matters affect the qualify of life. The more human ecology concerns itself with the quality of life, the more of a social study it becomes, involved with matters quite outside the normal range of the natural sciences.

The earthworm, to the best of my knowledge, is incapable of asking himself such questions as: "Do I want to make vegetable mould?" "Do I like my environment?" "How could it be improved?" The human equivalent of the earthworm not only is perfectly capable of asking all these questions, if he is an ecologist he does ask them. Indeed a good deal of the subject matter of the discipline seems to start from such questions.

Since so much of the human environment is the work of man, there is some point in asking them. If man can alter his environment once, he can alter it again, if only by undoing what he has already done; it is unlikely that all his deeds will be irreversible. There is also good reason to pose these questions because so much of the man-made environment — such as the noise and the pollution — is quite clearly harmful to man, and because there is no guarantee that the environment will maintain man at the standard to which he has become accustomed or to which he aspires.

Human ecologists have a range of environmental targets which are wholly admirable. They want to avoid starvation, they oppose the waste of materials, they oppose noise, pollution, inequity, they want an environment which is easy on, more than that, which stimulates the nerves, body and spirit of man.

It is when they come to discuss specific problems and propose solutions to them that they, or at least some of them, appear to me to be inadequate. I have heard an ecologist talking of promoting equity in human society with an airy confidence which suggested that he was unaware that this is a business which has been exercising some elements in society for some hundreds of years, without as much success as one would like. No matter; for him, apparently, equity is something which can be launched on society like a new model of a motor car. *Égalité* today; *liberté* and *fraternité* in the weeks to come. I understand there is a proposal afoot to deal with the noise and fumes of motor cars by stopping the building of roads, to drive people back into public transport. The solution has the ruthless simplicity of the universal remedy which the queen offered in *Alice in Wonderland* — "Off with his head!" Ruthless simplicity characterizes more than one ecological solution. Urban development, for example, is discussed as if the only matters to be considered are pollution, health and the larger crime rate of the big cities. An improved quality is to be brought into life by transforming society into a mosaic of relatively tiny communities; there is an echo here of the community of New Harmony which Robert Owen, capitalist and trade unionist, launched with a notable absence of success in the United States in the nineteenth century. At times, honest simple toil in a peaceful rural environment has an appeal to most of us; in practice it is likely to contain too much sweat, poverty and boredom. In some respects these ecologists remind me of the well-intentioned people who tried to improve the quality of life in the United States by prohibiting alcohol, an act which did nothing to diminish the attractions of the demon drink, though it gave a sizeable boost to gangsterdom. A ban on motor cars might not lead to a market in bootleg pollution, though it might lead to a massive objection to ecologists and all their works.

Perhaps there is an element of pique behind these remarks. In a recent newspaper article, an ecologist extended an invitation to scientists, other academics, industralists and trade unionists to assist in solving the population problem. We have heard of the unhappy man who took his harp to the party but nobody asked him to play. The economists were not even specifically invited to this party, though its avowed purpose was to evolve a new socio-economic system. The sociologists were not invited either. For me at least the blow was softened by the fact that I have been invited to your party. Nevertheless, the lack of interest in what the economist might have to say is disappointing in view of the fact that what some of the more vocal ecologists are saying in 1972 bears a striking resemblance to what one of the founding fathers of economics, the Rev. T. Malthus, said in 1798. Economists were interested in environmentalist matters before Darwin ever saw the *Beagle*. As long ago as 1776, Adam Smith remarked on the relationship between a man's environment and his productive efficiency: "that men in general should work better when they are ill-fed than when they are well fed, when they are disheartened than when they are in good spirits, when they are frequently sick than when they are generally in good health, seems not very probable".[1] With the prudence he admired, Adam Smith did not commit himself very far, though he ran counter to the practice of his own and later years; but whatever its quality, his remark, I submit, is the remark of an ecologist. The utopian socialists of the early nineteenth century — more economists — were especially conscious of the defects of the man-made environment. Thus Saint-Simon on equity: "Society is a world which is upside down. The nation holds as a fundamental principle that the poor should be generous to the rich, and that therefore the poorer classes should daily deprive themselves of necessities in order to increase the superfluous luxuries of the rich".[2] Or Sismondi who, before the railway age let alone the jet age, summoned the friends of humanity to slow down the pace of living, to assist "in retarding the social chariot which, in its accelerated course, seems to be on the point of plunging us into the abyss".[3] And finally the eminent late Victorian economist Alfred Marshall, whose views on the potential uses of the environment included a range of possibilities more extensive, I imagine, than are possessed nowadays by those who regard themselves as very thorough-going ecologists. "... the chief importance of material wealth". wrote Marshall, "lies in the fact that, when wisely used, it increases the health and strength, physical, mental and moral of the human race".[4]

Economics is in fact a study of the social environment. It is concerned with man cast in the dominant role of decision-maker on what is to be done with the resources with which his environment provides him. Economics is concerned with the satisfaction of man's wants by the goods and services which can be obtained from the raw materials and labour present in his environment. More precisely, the aspect of this matter which is the province of economics is the consequences in connection with human satisfaction which flow from three facts: the fact that there is no end to people's wants for goods and services, the fact that, in contrast, the environmental resources are limited, the fact that these resources for the most part can be used to satisfy wants in a variety of ways.

Because of these three facts it follows that the available quantity of a material can be used to make a range of commodities, but the more of the material that is used in the production of one commodity, the less remains for the production of others. Therefore mankind, with its endless list of wants, is forced to decide what it wants most of all, which normally leads to a decision to have a certain combination of finite quantities of certain goods, a combination which it prefers to any other combination.

The inevitability of choice leads the economist into a consideration of the nature of the value which people attach to goods and services, and so to a consideration of the influences which determine the prices of goods and services and the wages, salaries, profits and rents of those involved in their provision. From these matters economics may conveniently be taken to proceed to certain aspects of production, such as the motivation of production, the optimum pattern of production as indicated by human wants, the costs of production, the various matters affecting the economic efficiency of production, which is measured by relating the value of what is put into a productive process to the value of what comes out of it.

Economics indicates the manner in which anticipated human satisfaction influences demand and so affects the production of goods and services. Goods are made, not because of the profligate wickedness of producers but because people want them; the proposition is shattering in its obviousness, but it is not so obvious that it is always remembered. Economics indicates the way in which the price mechanism relates demand to supply: if demand increases, price tends to rise, which in turn will tend to stimulate production. But the price mechanism works equally well the other way round; if supplies are scarce, price will tend to rise, which in turn will tend to cut down demand.

Economics also has a great deal to say about the profit motive and its effect on production. Economists have never regarded the profit motive as being morally attractive, nor have they made selfish men their ideal, though they have often been accused of doing so. Adam Smith saw the profit motive as a beneficial force in society, but only in the sense that it led people to give better service to the community because that way lay a better chance of profit for themselves. Later economists would still subscribe to Smith's views, whilst admitting that there are other less commendable ways of adding to profits, such as by restricting supply, or by minimizing costs of getting rid of unwanted by-products by simply releasing them on the community as pollution.

Economics includes the study of production directed not by private considerations of profit but by decisions of a State planning organization. Such an economy has no profit reason to avoid paying the true costs of production by omitting the costs of dealing properly with pollution. The practice, as revealed by economic history, the auxiliary of economics, is not quite so satisfactory. It depends on the priorities of the planners who, though for other reasons, may be as little perturbed about pollution as the worst of capitalists. Not only that, in practice production in response to physical targets — so many tons of this, so many yards of that — can lead to the production of some very unwanted goods. The economic history of the U.S.S.R. is full of such examples. Directors have sought to fulfil the letter of their obligations with as little inconvenience to themselves as possible. A lampshade factory, given the target of so many lampshades, eased the problem by making them all the same colour. A cement block factory given a target expressed in numbers of blocks, concentrated on producing small blocks; given a target in tons, concentrated on big ones; in both cases regardless of the sizes the users of cement blocks required. As manufacturers of cement blocks, their job was to fulfil, better overfulfil, their target; what could be done with the resultant product was not their business.

Lower costs of production open the way to lower prices to consumers and to increased consumer satisfaction. Economics shows that costs of production can be reduced by siting a factory in this place rather than that because of savings in respect to the cost of materials, power, access to markets and the like. Division of labour also saves costs; that is, the practice of dividing the process of manufacture into a series of separate tasks of which an individual worker is called on to perform only one or two; he or she, may for example spend his working life putting lids on tins of cocoa. This makes the worker economically more productive in that it costs less to teach him a few skills than a lot; he can concentrate on work within his capacity, the less capable not being called upon to essay feats which they can hardly manage and the more capable being fully used; he has too the opportunity of acquiring quite abnormal proficiency at his work through constant practice. There are savings in cost to be made by increasing the scale of production, because that allows for more division of labour and for the use of a greater range of specialised machinery, or for bigger, more expensive, but more efficient machines. An increase in the size of the company (which is a matter separate from the size of the factories, the actual producing units) gives scope for other economies, such as rebates on the price of the raw materials which are bought, because of the size of the the order, or the less reputable economies to be derived from the possession of the power to twist other people's arms. It should be added that economists know that these advantages do not go on forever: sooner or later, increase in scale increases rather than diminishes costs.

There are a number of points on the economist's study of wages and salaries to which I would like to draw your attention. If a man is paid more than the value of what he produces there may be a waste of labour because he may have no incentive to move to more valuable but (to him) no more remunerative work. If the wages of the unskilled are little different from the wages of the skilled, people may cease to make the effort to become skilled. Higher wages can cut down demand so much that a worker gets unemployment, not a rise in the standard of living, from an increase in wage rates. Economics, however, does not consist of an assortment of reasons for paying workmen as little as possible. Economics includes the point that people are customers as well as workers: the higher the wages they receive, the more purchasing power they bring to the market.

These snippets of economic thinking are intended to prove the truth of a number of points which I would like to make on the value of economics to the human ecologist. The ecologist is well aware of certain of the defects in the man-made environment, more aware than is the economist because of his knowledge of biology. Economics can help him to a more thorough understanding of the human environment by making him more aware of some of its merits. The man-made environment has provided more than pollution and waste; it has provided greater quantities and a greater range of goods and services for the satisfaction of mankind than would be possible without it. There are various mechanisms in human society which function better than some ecologists seem to realize. The profit motive can produce service as well as pollution. The price mechanism is not merely an obscene device which stimulates a headlong rush into filth and waste; if scarcity increases and prices are left free, prices will rise and progressively tend to put a brake on both population and consumption. Our present socio-economic system has more flexibility than it has been given credit for; it does not depend on expansion in the sense that it will not work without expansion. It works more sweetly to our liking in expansion, but it can cope with contraction too, though not as well as one would like. Incidentally, economists, most eminently the late Lord Keynes, have long been engaged with the problem of how to modify the socio-economic system so that it can cope with depression and instability in a less painful, more satisfactory manner.

Economics should also help the ecologist to a better understanding of how many-sided, complex and integrated a thing the human environment is. At an earlier stage I cited the proposition that goods are produced because they are wanted. This simple truth seems not to have been appreciated by the ecologists who thought that a solution to the fumes and noise of motor cars could be found in simply discouraging their use. This would certainly add to the quality of life by reducing the fumes and noise, but it would deduct from the quality of life by removing the satisfaction derived from the motor cars. No doubt, some of us have deplorable tastes, and should not take such vulgar pleasure in getting a little ahead of the Joneses, but that is a reason for further education — not for driving us willy-nilly into an aseptic prison. If there is no joy, there is no quality of living. There is the same complexity in connection with production. The economies of production may increase the amount of noise to which the worker is subjected, bore him with the monotony of cocoa tin lids, dishearten him by increasing his sense of being merely a small cog in a big machine, encourage the growth of large urban agglomerations despite their higher crime rates, but they also cheapen production and to this extent make greater consumer satisfaction possible. Similarly wages. Fairness is not simply and satisfactorily achieved by giving more to the poorer paid. Thereby one may be unfair to the man who has painfully acquired a special skill; one may be creating unemployment and discouraging the acquisition of skills.

This is not to say that the role of economics is to prove to the human ecologist that this is the best of all possible worlds and that he would be well advised to pipe down and go home. If I may be a little blunt, the role of economics in the field of human ecology is to take the nonsense out of ecology and let its merits prevail.

References
1 A. Smith: The Wealth of Nations, Bk.I, chap.8.
2 F. M. H. Markham: Henri, Comte de Saint-Simon, Selected Writings.
3 J. C. de Sismondi: Études sur l'Économie Politique, Vol.II, p.211.
4 A. Marshall: Principles of Economics, 6th edition, Bk.IV, chap.5, p.193.

Discussion

J. O. Jones, Commonwealth Bureau of Agricultural Economics. On the question of the position of economics in human ecology, participants might be interested in a survey conducted among the members of the Commonwealth Human Ecology Council (CHEC) to determine which subjects they considered to be central and peripheral to human ecology. The results were as follows. Subjects regarded as central were economics, biology, geography, sociology, medicine, public health and nutrition, anthropology and demography. Peripheral subjects came out as architecture, political science and technology (including "intermediate technology"). Permeating both groups were agriculture, land use and town and country planning, education and philosophy, especially theory of values. In the present context it is significant that economics was regarded by this group, the members of CHEC, as particularly important.

M. J. L. Hussey. While I agree that there is a job to be done by economists (and others) in knocking some of the nonsense out of the looser talk about ecology, there is also a need to knock a lot of nonsense out of economics. To this end I would like to make the following five points:

1. It is not a valid generalisation to say that goods are made because they are wanted. In industrialised countries a very substantial proportion of goods are wanted because they are made. The making of wants is itself a large industry.

2. The profit-motive may have one merit in that, given that society is too complex to be regulated by a rule-book, it does appear to have a crudely homeostatic function. But the important question is - is the quest for profitability beneficial in achieving optimal allocations of resources? I don't think we can afford much longer to deceive ourselves that this is so.

3. It is ludicrous to warn of dangers of misallocating resources when every day confronts us with overwhelming evidence of misallocation. Why pretend that theoretical constructs like *Pareto-optima* based on marginal-cost pricing bear even a remote resemblance to reality. Prices are not determined in this way for industrial products — the reality is 'cost-plus' or 'what the market will bear'. We really need not worry about disturbing an ideal system that we haven't got.

4. It will not do to reject all notions of the planning of resource use by pointing up defects in centrally planned economies. Of course, there are difficulties, and great ones, but the exposure of faults should help to cure them. The faults of our profit-motivated economy despite their glaringly obvious nature, are apparently very easily ignored!

5. The previous point is not doctrinaire (as opposition to it appears to be) but has significant consequences for irreplaceable resources. Consider North Sea gas — a resource that can be made available only by heavy capital investment. When its use is governed by commercial criteria — as is the case for British nationalised industries — there is only one way that the return on the committed capital can be raised to the level demanded by the doctrine of profitability. That is to use up the gas as fast as possible (provided of course that sufficient demand can be created to keep the price up). Every resource is subject to the same goads to profligacy.

G. A. Petch. While accepting Professor Hussey's first point in the initial stages of the development of a market for, say colour television sets, one cannot go on with that situation indefinitely. Creating a demand acts as a kind of self starter, but in the long term a particular product will be produced because it is wanted.

On the regulatory effects of profits, I would not suggest that the profit motive is a perfect guide, and where it does not function effectively then some form of social planning will indeed be necessary.

Concerning labour allocation, there is no doubt that the present system is imperfect. The problem is how to find a better system, but I would not accept that, for example, the centrally planned economies have a better system.

On your last point, I agree about our present imperfect system in this country; there certainly is room for improving that system.

6

A Geographer's Viewpoint

H. BOWEN-JONES

"The question of questions for mankind . . . is the ascertainment of the place which Man occupies in nature and of his relations to the universe of things. Whence our race has come; what are the limits of our power over nature, and of nature's power over us; to what goal we are tending; are the problems which present themselves anew and with undiminished interest to every man born into the world".

Thus wrote T. H. Huxley one hundred and ten years ago. One hundred years before this English biologist was seeking a philosophy which could embrace a scientifically rigorous understanding of man's place in the universe, Immanuel Kant was seeking, through geography, the empirical knowledge to assist his philosophical exploration of the relationship between man and the physical universe.

I have indulged in this scholarly name-dropping in order to make my first preliminary point, namely that for a hundred and fifty years or so scientific and philosophical method and inquiry have frequently been allies in the search for understanding the interfacial zone between man and what we have learnt to call his environment. Before this time we find centuries of general speculation, description and assertion, sometimes intelligent, often superficial. For over a century, however, intellectual integrity has demanded that rigorous logic and scientific experimental proof be utilised in our quest for knowledge in this field. Superficiality too often still remains but now it is perhaps our own fault if we suffer it.

Both Huxley and Kant were, among other things, pedagogues. To each of them it appeared a duty to convey, not only to full-time students but also to others, including the policy makers and decision takers of their day, a sense of the relevance of holism and the necessity for scholarly evaluation and appraisal. The one great difference between their approach and ours is that they were almost entirely concerned with understanding for its own sake whereas we are additionally concerned with the application of such understanding, through both positive and negative action, in order to — and here you have a personal choice, akin to that of choosing to describe a container as half-empty or half-full —

to extricate mankind (or some men) from a human (or specific) predica- ment or to improve generally and/or specifically the quality of human life. This is our end and our goal.

At this conference we are in particular concerned with the educating of human ecologists, this being one means to our end.

What, however, can we learn from the happenings of this last period of exploration? The first moral is perhaps a cautionary paradox. Since evolutionary biology joined the scientific ranks of mathematics, chemistry and physics, since the physiocrats introduced the concept of "natural order" and political economy to the family of history and philosophy, there has been a continuous breeding of specialisations. Of the subjects now listed in the curricula of institutions of higher educa- tion almost two-thirds were born after 1870 and the process of con- tinuous creation seems still to continue. Yet, simultaneously with the procreation of esoteric skills, each highly involved and often mutually incomprehensible, one finds at the top, in this area of man-in-the- universe, a remarkable vanishing of compartment walls, a discarding of labels.

An economist may use terms such as "the importance of external diseconomies" while a biologist may refer to an "ecological law of the inoptimum"; at a certain level however the similarity of problem identification produces a lingua franca. It may be worth considering that this for the most part comes with age and experience; this was the traditional and often valid main reason for arranging for professors to teach freshers and exposing senior students to the newly-fledged PhD. This type of common language is also most easily achieved between specialists during research rather than instruction.

There have been of course some movements towards the grouping of some subjects in new disciplines but of these as yet only one, geography, has deliberately insisted on concerning itself centrally with the mutual relationships between human and non-human phenomena, dynamic and spatially variable relationships. I am not here to make any grandiose claims for geography but if any should doubt the truth of this assertion let him consider why geography makes a nonsense of Dewey-based decimal library classifications, why geography is so often found at one and the same time in faculties and research councils of arts, science and social science, why in every one of the Commonwealth groups appearing spontaneously and in response to the efforts of CHEC, in the field of human ecology *there* are the geographers in action.

Our experience even in geography however has been, as I have said elsewhere, that "matters of emphasis, significant details of balance become causes of argument. The impossibility of being a polymath without being a charlatan rapidly leads to sub-specialisation and this in turn leads to a differentiation between schools of thought". I believe that our experience in this discipline (which out of the over 70 subject categories in which student applications are listed by the University Central Council on Admissions has been in the top five ever since records commenced) only serves to confirm an inevitable tendency towards this natural sort of specialisation. Here again it is true that mutual comprehensibility between specialists increases with age and experience and is most easily achieved "in the field", particularly in what we may call applied research.

If then in the education of ecologists we are attracted not merely by the necessity for holistic understanding and appreciation but by the possibility of devising curricula which are in fact holistic, I would suggest that we should stop and ask ourselves why specialisation and sub-specialisation has hitherto been the natural order of the day. That this latter process has not been wholly good for the world of education is no doubt true and that, as Sir Hugh Springer, Chairman of CHEC and Secretary General of the Association of Commonwealth Universities asserted at the first International Conference of Human Ecology: "In educational circles in the more developed countries there is evidence of increasing dissatisfaction with the excessive dominance of the "subject" . . .". If, however, because we associate the dominance of the "subject", often correctly no doubt, with the blinkered compartmentalisation of knowledge and therefore also of understanding, we wish to replace it with something better then I would suggest that something more than enthusiasm is required.

The first pre-requisite is a simple sense of reality. No matter what level or type of education is concerned there are a finite number of hours in a working day and days in a week and weeks in a year and years in a learner's life. As people concerned with human ecology we are very apt to insist on the finiteness of the world's material resources and equally apt to forget that the most easily destroyed and only impossible-to-substitute resource is time itself. We all in reality know this. No matter how strong a case of academic desirability may appear to be, the ultimate, immovable object in education is the timetable. The more advanced the process the more frustrating this can be. One or two simple examples will illustrate this point. As a geographer, and this happens to all my colleagues, I frequently find myself on committees considering new inter-disciplinary courses. Most recently this involved Colleges of Education and a deceptively simple proposal called "Local Studies". Interested participants included historians, biologists, theologians, economists as well as geographers but no-one had any illusions that this gave anything more than partial coverage. What very rapidly appeared was that if students devoted approximately twice as much time to this course as they would to any other, if members of staff devoted about three times as much of their time (most of it in inter-communication and organisation) as they would to any other, then a not unreasonable partial picture could appear of *some* of the linkages, the

inter-related processes, the understanding of which might — but only if
the balance was right — clarify the appreciation of a few small areas.
That this was worth doing I have no doubt. That it was not feasible,
ultimately because of the scale of input demands, became equally
obvious.

If, however, the input demands had been acceptable, the return
would not have been at a very professional level; that is, if the purpose
was elevated to the training of people professionally qualified directly
to intervene in the processes which make even a micro-region much
more would be needed. Let us merely consider one small aspect of the
work required, for example, reading of the relevant literature. Assume
for a moment that a student may be expected in addition to other
working activities to spend, most improbably, 20 hours a week in reading and digesting what he has read and that this, at an unlikely maximum
of 50 weeks a year, allows 1000 hours of concentrated consumption.
This would allow him or her in that time to cover the literature produced
in the field of environmental perception in the last five years in English
alone — with all the parochialism which that implies. Presumably there
would be a little time later to look at one or two minor aspects of the
environment itself!

This is so patently absurd that it would seem that I have merely set
up a conveniently vulnerable Aunt Sally. This, however, is far from my
intention. I am solely concerned with the fact that, *qua* geographer,
some twenty-five years' experience has proved to me that once one
enters the world of "man-in-environment" it is a world of maximum
complexity in which every problem is multi-variate.

The joint dilemma of time-restriction and immensity of knowledge
is of course one with which teachers of all sorts are familiar and, in
practice, we find working compromises. The first of these is to concentrate effort at the level of principle. Here the skill, knowledge and
maturity of the instructor become critical factors, particularly so because
the instructor becomes the dominating, the key factor in what to the
student can be a labyrinthine situation. This is not a simple matter of
more contact hours of teaching. Since one of our basic premises is that
knowledge-based holistic understanding has, through education, to be
added to whatever innate capabilities of ecological appreciation which
man possesses, it necessarily follows that the more multi-variate the
discipline, the more tortuous — even tenuous — becomes the path of
learning. If this is to be followed successfully then the student has to
place an enormous amount of trust in his teachers, in the system, trust
that the relevance of what at early stages may appear to be an assemblage
of not totally necessary or conceptually associated work, will eventually
appear. From research evidence and personal experience we all know
that this always to some extent is true; we also know that it becomes
critical whenever the conceptual range and the volume of required fact

becomes great, when the blinkers of personal experience are forced apart and the work load is increased. There is also the little matter of trust that the teacher, the instructor is right, that his evaluations are correct, that his judgement is sound.

Once again this is a normal situation except for two factors; the first being the difficulty which the learner finds at the level of principle in this field (because of time and complexity), of developing, on the basis of independent work, valid judgement criteria of his own: the second is that since the desirability of educating human ecologists arises from a sense of urgency and of the importance attached to this field then we cannot afford many mistakes. *"Quis custodiet . . ."*, the old maxim, is terribly apposite when we consider the training of some who will be the guardians of the human heritage. There is too much at stake for us to be content either with arguments which are elegant but wrong or with uninformed (and therefore inapplicable) idealism.

The second type of working compromise with which we are familiar in education is that of combining a considerable amount of general principle with as much as possible of specialised knowledge and experience. As usual, as we know from a variety of experience, this has both advantages and drawbacks. In the University teaching of geography, itself possessing many multi-disciplinary characteristics, many departments including my own find it very valuable to encourage students to choose some specialised thematic courses such as ecology and conservation, urban geography and planning, agriculture and development etc., special optional fields studied in some depth concurrently with courses which all students take in common. Many other disciplines adopt similar procedures but in every case the effectiveness of this approach varies with the strength or weakness of the central ethos. In human ecology a considerable amount of hard thinking is urgently needed so that a working consensus may. be established concerning what this central ethos really is.

I am not being obstructionist when I say that this itself is not going to be an easy matter, particularly in the context of education. How far are we agreed that at the centre of our whole concept stands man and that our criteria for judging ecological long term stability are determined by human aspirations including the survival of the human species? Many people apparently equally concerned with matters ecological, view this approach with horror as being anthropocentric to a degree which invalidates it both intellectually and in practical application. How far are we prepared to accept the logical implications of a man-centred stand-point? Even if we accept a hypothetical "human ecologists' man" are we prepared fully to consider what we know and, equally important, what we do not know of his rich complexity? At a CHEC Commonwealth Symposium last November I suggested that: "The potential contribution of social psychology to development policy evaluation is vast but is at the moment pathetically inadequate". This is even more true in the context of the kind of social and environmental engineering to which the education of human ecologists is relevant. As yet, to be brutally frank, we of the materially affluent world have done little more than arrive by accident and by various paths at a twentieth century Wailing Wall where we bemoan the future loss of paradise, a paradise moreover which has no consistent structure but which is variously fashioned according to our several predilections and backgrounds. Also according with our various specialist fields of knowledge are our differently weighted plans for avoiding a global catastrophe which itself may come in any of several ways, each of which is gloomily claimed by its partisans to be the only true road to ruin.

This may appear intellectual masochism and to some extent this is so. Above this however rises the clear unshakeable fact that appears from any review of the present flood of literature, sound and unsound, concerning the human predicament. The fact is that beyond a realisation (which has come later to some than to others and to many not at all), that a tight web of inter-relationships binds together everything in and on earth — and perhaps beyond — beyond this, we are not yet agreed which sets of strands, which interfaces are most critically significant. Moreover, to establish such agreement will require hard work and humility.

To return for a moment to T. H. Huxley. "In scientific inquiry it becomes a matter of duty to expose a supposed law to every possible kind of verification, and to take care, moreover that this is done intentionally, and not left to a mere accident". To a biologist of any sort along with chemists and physicists, pedologists and engineers this is obviously true and feasible but what of the anthropologists and psychologists over much of their fields, or the economists, sociologists, theologians and historians? Even geologists and architects are frequently unable to replicate experiments. Geographers have lived with this problem for long, operating both in the world of deliberate experimental verification and in that in which reliance has to be placed on correlation and network analysis, utilising data from situations which exist rather than have been "set up". In the sort of overseas development work which involves me as researcher and as consultant it is rare not to have to utilise both approaches. From this the major lesson we have learnt is that the environment is a subjective as well as an objective reality. As the latter it can be measured and analysed — with regionally varying degrees of difficulty. This however is not enough since it is not "man" but particular groups of and individual men and women who subjectively observe and evaluate and then interact with the objective environmental reality in highly complex and far from uniform ways. If we see the need for applied human ecology arising from a global situation then we must eschew the arrogance born of uniformitarianism based on *our* experience and learn, as so many of us have had to do, to appreciate the rationale of regional variations in the dynamic inter-relationship of man and environment. So much for the central ethos which, if strong, can maintain a centripetal hold on partial specialists. What of the fields of special knowledge which we may invite students to explore? I would suggest that they fall into three main groups, biological, cultural and technological. Further break-down would depend on the nature of the central common curriculum but the fundamental problem would remain that of providing an opportunity to master some particular specialisms to a demonstrably useful level while at the same time avoiding the compartmentalisation effect of specialisation; the other demands of reasonableness of time and energy input and of high quality of instruction would of course still exist.

At this point it becomes clearly necessary to consider who is to be educated and for what purpose, since, given some apparent urgency and, as we insist, limited and finite resources, our educational investment must be designed for maximum effectiveness. There is a fairly simple dichotomy here with which we are sufficiently familiar, that between the planners and the planned or the doctors and the doctored. Let us first consider the latter group.

Ideally, every planner, every doctor hopes that the patient will be responsive and responsible — "awareness" is too woolly to serve. In development work it becomes absolutely clear that this matter of response is vital to the success of any project: among the many reasons for failure, the absence of preparation of people at grass-root level for project implementation looms surprisingly large. If applied human ecology is to increase intervention in people's lives, both positively and negatively, then this intervention will be ineffective unless the desired response is forthcoming. I would suggest therefore that a pre-requisite for success is the injection into general education, and here I mean at school level and wherever possible also in adult education and information, of courses and material designed to instil ecologically sensible attitudes.

What is possible, particularly if we are at this level prepared to accept the honest word "indoctrination", is to design one or two basic courses — as compulsory as religious or physical education — in which, in the context of man's life on this earth, the essential matter of interlocking cause and effect is demonstrated. (The context implies of course the involvement of human and non-human phenomena.) In relatively specialised fields the Royal Society junior lectures-cum-demonstrations are excellent examples of one way in which this kind of thing can be done: they also suggest to me that this kind of indoctrination of basic truths is only effective as well as ethical if it is done well, if the intention is honest and if the truths are genuine.

The dangers of such action are of course enormous and only justified if the dangers of not acting are even greater. It may be felt that education, formal and informal, should not contain elements of indoctrination, of attitude moulding, of this kind. This particular pass is however already sold, sold moreover in some highly dangerous ways. At the informal level, and this is true in all but the remotest micro-societies, we are already subjected to an almost continuous injection of propaganda material of all kinds by the so-called mass media, the only variations appearing in the degree and the purposes to which this influence is consciously manipulated. If we regard applied human ecology as necessary and urgently desirable then we must face up to this challenge. The degree of urgency involved in the human predicament becomes itself of major importance; if the catastrophists are right then ethical objections to brain-washing lose much of their strength — only a fool disputes authority on a sinking ship. If however we have a little more time then it is vital, for the sake of man himself and for the whole range of communities of men, that what we inculcate is right in as many respects as possible.

Proceeding on the second assumption concerning the time at our disposal let me illustrate briefly by two examples just what I mean. The first has to do with societies such as ours, relatively affluent and specialist-structured in all possible ways from material production to religious organisation. These are the societies in which now there is a clarion call "What has gone wrong?" — and I quote from a publishers brochure on a recent American work. We are apparently over-producing and over-consuming and in the wrong ways; we are changing our environment (we cannot destroy it), and many of the new features are disliked. What however is the constructive educational message that must be implanted and who is to be responsible for its implantation?

For all who have completed their formal education we presumably have to do two rather different things, first, produce programmes suitable for the significant minority who voluntarily participate in adult education schemes and, secondly, devise information and orientation programmes to which the others will be exposed. It is most important that we take this adult level of education seriously and also acknowledge its difficulties. Its seriousness is associated with biological and acculturation time-lag. The first of these is illustrated in the recent first report of the President's Commission on Population Growth and the American Future; even on the basis of an average two child family the American population will increase by one-third in the next thirty years and nothing except major calamity will prevent it. The acculturation factor is clear to any one who has carried out any investigation in social and/or economic fields; major behavioural changes generally take generations rather than years. We cannot wait therefore for new formal educational programmes for the young to have their effect. The difficulties remain and I would suggest that they present a challenge which should squarely be met by crash programmes of research and trial by those who are competent to do so.

The difficulties are partly inherent, partly associated with this matter of competence. The inherent problem is that, no matter for the moment why, so-called "Western" man as Boeke pointed out thirty years ago has developed virtually limitless powers of consumption; he has now to learn to impose or have imposed on himself considerable limitations. Growthmanship for its own sake is apparently discredited but just try convincing people on the Upper Clyde or North East or South West England that the gods of wealth are false gods. Are the Aberdonians wrong to exult in the oil and gasfield boom which they are beginning to experience? Can Venice be saved without the creation of wealth?

In what loosely may be called the West, much of the anti-rat-race propaganda to which the adult population is subjected lacks consistency. An example of this was seen when, on one and the same day a few months ago, it was possible to receive four television programmes, the first containing a diatribe about packaging, the second stressing the importance of protecting foodstuffs against contamination; a little later the British motor vehicle industry was castigated for its apparent inability globally to compete in producing goods which in a still later programme were described as producing the ruination of society. Heaven forbid that there should be totally guided consistency of an authoritarian kind but the confusion which can be caused by such contradictions is hardly likely to produce an ecologically responsive and responsible public.

The other danger is simple backlash. In February, during the Tennant Memorial Lecture to the Society of Chemical Industry, Dr. Hessayon said this: "Chemistry and industry have transformed the world into a place where man can expect to live a full 70-year lifespan. Now man is at risk and ironically the risk is greatest from just those people who are so loudly talking about the balance of nature . . .". "Public and political pressures should not be allowed to decide major scientific issues — the public has neither the expert knowledge nor the time to sort and weigh the evidence".

This kind of reaction which is vocal and powerful at many levels, institutional, in local and national government as well as industry, is provoked essentially in situations of confrontation and made possible by the spurious simplification of complex matters. Man-in-the-street reaction is quite simply either cynicism or confusion. If we are to have a society in which sensible attitudes in matters of human ecology are sufficiently strong to ensure a reasonable public response to policy measures, are even strong enough to make such measures politically desirable, then we must design and put into action sensible and effective adult education measures, both formal and informal. This matter is too important to be left solely to the present range of mass-media services.

In the less developed world, and this has appeared quite strikingly in previous CHEC conferences, post-school education in human ecology has to have a different balance. Given that the greatest need now becomes the raising of living standards in all possible ways since, however ardently we may romanticise the simple life, we cannot believe that poverty, disease and illiteracy are good, given this the emphasis presumably must be placed on educating the masses to development with different expectations from those which have become normal in the affluent world. The implications of this are of course enormous and any consequent decisions are the responsibility of the societies concerned. One measure of the seriousness with which this responsibility is being taken is the proliferation of population-planning policies in the less developed countries. One word of caution however. In its anxiety to avoid some of the ecological mistakes made by the richer countries, the developing world must beware turning its back on the technological and conceptual experience which they possess. We in turn must not export too many features of our currently fashionable guilt-complex.

I have spent most of my time dealing with general issues and the challenge of public education, the geographical contribution appearing mainly by implication. The justification for this lies in our normal tendency to concentrate on more formal processes and also in the urgency of the situation. Formal education of the relatively young I shall consider with some brevity, first because much of what I have already said is equally relevant here, secondly because, while I would suggest that some guide-lines can be derived from geographical experience, this is a field in which it is easier to make headlines than rapid progress.

Any educational system has three main chronological components, school (junior and senior), undergraduate (and equivalent), and postgraduate. School curricula are designed for the education of those who continue with later studies and for those who do not. The latter, the great but decreasing majority, cannot be given comprehensive courses of any depth in human ecology, but require something more than classroom platitudes. The opportunities and needs at elementary and secondary level urgently require collaborative research and design by teams of educationists and human ecological specialists operating at national level if future generations are at least to be inculcated with rational ecological attitudes. Since so many of these attitudes are little more than extensions of simple truths not wholly popular today, such as the linkage of action and consequence, the fact that "doing your own thing" invariably has some nasty repercussions, or the fallacy of the Platonic doctrine of reminiscence — that people know everything at birth and become progressively more ignorant as they grow older — the official acceptance of recommendations will itself not be easy to achieve.

Other school courses would be necessary for the ever-growing minority of young people who will proceed to some form or other of higher education, of whom a small proportion might become professional human ecologists. The education of the last small group might be considered the *raison d'être* of this conference but I hope that we shall not confine our attention to it. The others, some vocationally trained, some not, will constitute the great bulk of our professionally trained cadres of the future, our doctors, civil engineers, accountants, social workers, industrial chemists, trade union leaders, air-line administrators, architects, diplomats, politicians — the list is endless. These together make up a key sector in almost every society now in existence; they are the specialists without which life would be nasty, brutish and short. Let us not fool ourselves with the myth of the noble savage. I spend much of my working life in relatively simple societies and have too high a regard for their virtues dishonestly to ignore their deficiencies; dominated by survival demands their concepts of quality of life are extremely limited. One thing which we can learn from comparative geographical knowledge is that societies without much structured specialisation offer fewer opportunities for human development than those which have built up such complexities and are no less destructive — only slower in action both for ill or good.

These professional specialists, which we already have in some strength and which the developing countries are perforce rapidly training, themselves require educating in the principles of human ecology and in the relevance of those principles to their own special skills. Here one is in a delicate area since the good specialist usually believes that he is already capable of seeing things holistically. Perhaps this led the ex-editor of the *Architectural Review* when speaking to the R.I.B.A. (reported in *The Times,* 15 March 1972) into complaining that a profession trained to become guardians of the environment was falling down on the job; led a well-known American biological ecologist to claim that the circle of life has been broken not by biological need but by other forces which by implication therefore are bad. We all recognise in these and a thousand other explicit or implicit claims our own specialist sins of pride, immensely dangerous because they go with the power and the authority necessarily vested in the expert. The only possible way I see of improving this situation through education is by being concertedly quite ruthless in criticism and equally vociferous in approval. Any course in higher education claiming to be concerned centrally with the inter-relationship of man and environment must either be honestly described as having certain deliberate limitations of coverage or be defensible in terms of comprehensive balance. Titles such as "Environmental Management" or "Human Ecology" should only be recognised on the showing of the signs of nobility. On the other hand I am equally sure that a great deal of approval could be given to the collaborative provision and acceptance of "service courses".

Would not there be at least some benefit to human ecology if specially designed courses in economics were taken by some doctors, in biology to be taken by some historians, in psychology by some architects? Already much apparently is being done in this direction; how much however is or could be done deliberately to make the specialist first aware of his ignorance of fields other than his own, secondly of the interweave of these fields with his own, and lastly of how to establish effective working relationships between them, all in the cause of the orchestration of soloists.

Lastly, the training of professional human ecologists. If all the other areas I have touched on appear demanding then this as the White Queen said makes other hills look like valleys. I must confess that the more I think about it as a comprehensive professional and vocational training the less certain I am of its feasibility or even desirability.

Some of the reasons for this are directly derived from the general propositions with which I started, in particular those to do with time and competence. Other doubts come more directly from my experience as a geographer, personal research and teaching experience and some knowledge of colleagues' work. There are only a few things I am sure about and I would ask you to consider them.

First, human ecology is holistic. There is no environment — in our sense — without man or man without environment. A human ecologist is therefore committed to the study and understanding of an immense network of phenomena and forces ranging from the non-sentient inorganic through the sentient organic to the immaterial and possibly spiritual. Secondly, we are profoundly ignorant of many of these phenomena and forces and therefore must be extremely careful about extrapolation. Thirdly, the relative significance of phenomena and forces alike is not spatially uniform except at an extremely simple level or in ideal models. Lastly, the professional human ecologist in spite of these difficulties, when he is trained will have, as his only *raison d'être,* career responsibilities in social and environmental engineering, responsibilities which I would be loth to trust even to a combination of Solomon and Einstein.

The matter of range and volume of all that is comprehended in human ecology is of first importance. Earlier I suggested that it could be subsumed under three content headings — biological, cultural and technological — but if we then analyse these we find that we are dealing with virtually everything. Can we seriously believe that it is possible to educate a professional human ecologist who is capable of effective work in all the fields represented? Take one restricted example, that of freshwater demand and supply in this country. An article of April 1971 unintentionally posed part of the problem with amazing naivety thus:

"At present sewage disposal is largely financed from the general rates and the rate support grants which central government gives to supplement them. This means that finance for sewage disposal has to compete with what is needed for more schools, houses, policemen, dustmen and many other services. In such a scramble, more money for sewage disposal has a low priority". Forget for the moment, not only the naivety of supposing that any need can be made non-competitive with other needs, but also the host of other technological factors involved. Can any single man however trained really resolve these priorities? As I think all geographers would insist, man is more than a biological phenomenon and as such needs as well as wants a great range of services over and above those which enable species survival. Requirements of the spirit, of the psyche and of the intellect are as important as those of the flesh, and we must understand the processes by which they become manifest at least as well as any others.

Any education given to a human ecologist must contain above all scholarly humility on the part of instructor and instructed. If for no other reason I would suggest that the teaching team be large and, given our compartmentalised starting point, widely multi-disciplinary, and that both instructor and instructed be regularly and firmly involved in applied research in real situations. This might avoid the sort of confusing situation which developed last autumn when Dr. Borlaug, Nobel prizewinner and a man of considerable eminence in the field not only of plant-breeding but of agricultural biology, was reported as saying "If agriculture is denied the use of fertilisers and chemicals like D.D.T. because of unwise legislation that is now being promoted by a powerful group of hysterical lobbyists who are provoking fear by predicting doom for the world through chemical poisoning then the world will be doomed not by chemical poisoning but from starvation" when Dr. Mansholt of the Common Market Commission was calling for "a phasing out of D.D.T.", and when Dr. Galley, W.H.O. consultant, reported to the British Pest Control Association that world usage of D.D.T. had been cut by half between 1963 and 1970 but there was still justification in using D.D.T. discriminately and that an unjustified D.D.T. scare resulted from an "ability to measure becoming confused with the importance of the result".

It is particularly important to have accurate information when discussing problems of world resource conservation. Non-renewable resources, as economic geographers have been saying for decades, are exhaustible. That is undeniable, and what matters then is the interpretation placed on the estimates of reserves and consumption, that is the time scale for the exhaustion of available resources and the feasibility of substitution.

In addition to the requirement of accuracy in estimating reserves, it is important that human ecologists, or anyone else, should not apply the inflexible analysis of the mathematician to statistics of this kind. For example, it is possible to plot a graph which shows a falling curve of oil reserves against time, and superimpose a curve of exponentially increasing consumption against time, to demonstrate that the curves intersect and reserves will be exhausted before the end of the century. But the validity of that analysis leans heavily on the assumptions that the available data is sufficiently accurate and that consumption will indeed increase exponentially, and that none of the parameters is likely to change in an unforeseen manner. That is not to say that such calculations can never have value, but simply that a considerable degree of caution must be exercised in the extrapolation of results.

This is because it is vitally important that those who wish to inform and educate as professionals should present real facts — any presentation of inaccurate data to and by human ecologists of (to pursue our example) fuel and energy reserves will merely lead to their counsel being ignored. We cannot afford to play with figures. Non-renewable resources are necessarily exhaustible, and what matters, as with all other elements of human ecology, is what man *does* both globally and in specific regions and communities. Not only must the trainee human ecologist get his global facts right, be educated in intellectual integrity, but he must also appreciate the rich regional variety of human values and needs. To stay for a moment with oil, there might very well be a case on many grounds for maintaining that we in Britain are extravagant in our consumption of fossil hydrocarbons. There is an equally good case on the other hand for Nigeria to maximise her rate of oil exploitation and sale on the grounds that only by massive and rapid injections of capital derived from oil revenue can that country hope to achieve a reasonably higher and stable quality of life for its people based on a diversified and stable use of rich potential resources. Even more strongly might Qatar maintain that, with little but petroleum and her potential human resource wealth, rapid exploitation of oil over twenty years with wise investment of resulting income in human potential through education and training would ultimately yield more in human happiness than a doubling or quadrupling the period and a halving or quartering of the rate of increment of possible investment revenue.

One of the main reasons why I am an active member of the Commonwealth Human Ecology Council is that I can see so much mutual benefit, greater in whole than the sum of its parts, by collaboration and experience-sharing by a diversity of peoples. Geography can encourage the humility which comes of trying to appreciate and respect values and needs other than those of one's own society. The trained human ecologist similarly must be educated not invariably to exalt his own or his instructor's concepts and judgements into universal truths but to discriminate between the few true general laws and the myriad of half-true precepts.

Given all this you can see why I have grave doubts about setting up at this time comprehensive and vocational training schemes for human ecologists as such. The mechanics of the operation are far from insuperable; multi-variate analysis and data-collection and retrieval systems become ever simpler and the capacity of the human brain is as yet considerably under-taxed. What remains is quality of judgement and if we really regard humanity as being at risk then we should beware the blithe handing of power over the future to any single group or profession.

As a geographer but also as other things I believe that for the foreseeable future we should aim in the education of human ecologists at three particular targets. First, in adult and in general school education, at achieving a reasonably high level of comprehension of those inter-relationships between man and his environment which are most relevant to real people. There is a very strong case for making suitable courses compulsory for all at school. Secondly, in higher education of all kinds, doing two things; negatively, preventing too much feed-back into school curricula of more special requirements of the type which have helped to make geography not as effective as it might have been, in inculcating general school interest in the man/environment interface; positively, making it necessary, for many professional qualifications, for students satisfactorily to undertake work which is designed to break down main divisive compartments. This in particular might, for example, mean that any social scientist would have to take some specially designed courses indicating the relevance of some aspects of life sciences and technology; the converse would of course also hold. This is not the old idea of joint or general studies; this would be a deliberate measure of widening blinkered vision in a particular way. In practice, this might mean lengthening courses; it would certainly raise some but not necessarily very great academic opposition. It will not happen everywhere at once but could be practicable in some places with the right atmosphere.

The third target is our pedagogic selves. If sound attitudes of human ecology are generally to be inculcated, if there are to be better career prospects for those students who in addition to learning the mastery of some craft have an understanding of how to apply that mastery in sound ecological ways, then we in turn must possess more mutual understanding than we do at present. The cross-fertilisation must begin at this senior level and requires work as well as good will. One thing which I have learnt, as a geographer in the field, in research and teaching, is that no human dilemma can be understood or solved by a humanist alone or a scientist alone. A human ecologist must be both; of accepted status perhaps in his main field but knowledgeable without conceit in the other. A biologist may rightly claim that all flesh is grass but must be prepared to accept that a historical geographer may know why in a particular place there is grass and not something else. All this may sound extremely leisurely. I would suggest that there is every reason for speed but not for haste, although this is not the time or place for arguing against pessimistic catastrophism. All I would suggest now is that if the global Cassandras and Jeremiahs are correct then it is already too late. In the words of Thurber:

"I don't understand", said the scientist, "why you lemmings all rush down to the sea and drown yourselves".

"How curious", said the lemming. "The thing I don't understand is why you human beings don't".

I think it is more sensible as well as more comforting to rest with the words of a recent Huxley, Julian, quoted by Dr. Barton Worthington at the Commonwealth Conference on Human Ecology sponsored by CHEC in Malta and in the spirit of CHEC as it has evolved over the years: "the glorious possibilities that are still latent in man". What we are considering is but one aspect of making the latent potent.

Discussion

C. D. Curling, King's College, London. In some ways your paper is more radical and pessimistic than others we have heard today. You appear to think that the education of human ecologists cannot be undertaken within the system of higher education which we have in this country and that we must change the system to one in which human ecologists can be educated. What kind of changes do you envisage?

H. Bowen-Jones. If we first consider vocational training, we are really talking in terms of producing "super-planners", and it might well be possible to develop first degree courses to this end, although it must be accepted that such a degree would be no more than a preliminary qualification, to be backed up by several years of experience and possibly postgraduate training. But such a degree will be multidisciplinary and will require a high level of teaching ability on the part of the teaching staff. The difficulty is that human ecology does involve an holistic outlook, an outlook which it is not easy to achieve within our educational system. If we had, for example, a more fluid system of higher education as in Denmark, then the situation would certainly be easier.

7

The Contribution of Anthropology to the Study of Human Ecology

V. G. SHEDDICK

The attempt to outline the contribution of anthropology to the study of human ecology runs into immediate difficulties. Neither "anthropology" nor "human ecology" readily identifies itself in straight forward terms.

Human Ecology

In broad terms, *ecology* still has the meaning given to it by its innovator, Haekel; it is the study of the relationships existing between organisms and their surroundings, both non-living and living. These relationships are very numerous. They involve different levels of inter-action, ranging from the physical and the chemical to the physiological and, in some cases, the psychological.

The role of the ecologist is that of identifying the many different strands at factors making up a given complex of co-activity and of being able to mobilise and integrate the expertise of relevant specialised departments of study. In this aspect of his work he has been somewhat picturesquely described as a "chartered libertine" (Macfadyen, 1963, xi). This image, in its archaic interpretation, allows us to see the ecologist as a man, freed from the bondage of subservience to a single discipline, roaming at will and seeking what he can from biology and physiology, physics and chemistry, geology and meteorology, and anthropology and sociology.

At the same time, the ecologist has to avoid being a partisan, resisting the temptation to find vital connexions in one or two personally favoured approaches. The environment for him is an intricate and diverse complex of reciprocating reactions which refuse to be confined within tidy academic categories.

Environments are obviously relative constructs. They can exist only in relation to some point of reference. We recognise this when we distinguish plant and animal ecology and likewise when we speak of human ecology. These referential variations imply that there is some parent concept of which the sub-divisions are all, in their several ways, an expression. In practice, this logical linkage is acknowledged reluctantly and sometimes even denied.

Human ecology seems to have acquired a bewildering range of interpretations. (Bates, 1953, 700; Gibbs & Martin, 1959). Some would have it to be little more than another name for human geography and, as such, to concern itself with either human habitats or with human economics. Others would like it to be a specialised social science. (Hawley, 1944, 399). Upon one thing only does there seem to be general agreement and that is that human ecology is concerned in some way with the *relationships* that exist between men and their environments. (Quin, 1940, 192). Conveniently, but no more precisely our symposium has adopted as its working definition the statement that human ecology embraces all the terms used to denote the study of man in relation to his environment.

Statements of the scope and content of human ecology, as here understood, are still relatively few. (Weiner, 1964; Boughey, 1971). The pioneer contribution is undoubtedly that of J. W. Bews (1935). Here we find a list of the relevant factors that provides a clear indication of the contribution expected from the science of man. First Bews is careful to point out that "the environment" of the human ecologist will itself usually include human beings other than those who may be the centre of particular study. He recognises that human ecology is not a simple juxta-positioning of "man" and a collection of non-human factors. It concerns a particular collection of human beings acting in a total setting which may well include other collections of men. Secondly, he shows that the study of man himself requires to be identified with human genetics, human physiology, the study of man's diseases and disabilities seen as apparent maladjustments to environment, and with human psychology. Finally, we are directed to consider human culture as the reflexion of man's domination of nature.

Anthropology

Human ecology appears to be interested in two facets of the study of man; with his biological processes and with his socio-cultural activities. From its inception, anthropology has attempted to represent the whole study of man by bringing together the various particular and partial studies of mankind, some biological, some behavioural and others cultural. In terms of the fashionable methods and speculative ideas of the nineteenth century, it sought to present a single account of human existence. It was an inclusive natural history of man.

As its individual specialisms progressed, refining their methods and amending their guiding principles, so anthropology fragmented. By 1948 it was necessary for Daryll Forde to make a plea for the re-integration of the anthropological disciplines. He proposed that anthropologists should be concerned with the connexions one to another of the different phases of human life. The anthropologist was urged to be aware of "biological, environmental, technological, demographic, economic and political factors and processes as successive series of determinants of form and function in human cultures, social systems and bodies of beliefs" (Forde, 1948, 4). In this statement we find another convenient list of the special areas of study which may contribute to human ecology. At the same time, the suggestion was made that a unitary anthropology could well be achieved by the recognition of the integrative function of the ecological approach. (*ibid*, 9).

Anthropology, regretfully, remains a fragmented discipline. Its biological facet hovers between being human biology and physical anthropology. Its remaining interests sometimes find an uneasy unity in being "socio-cultural".

Physical anthropology has had a fairly constant identification with the tasks of tracing the course of human evolution and with seeking valid ways of differentiating the species in terms of significant criteria. At the same time its research strategy has moved forward from the initial, fact gathering, descriptive phase to a new level of activity directed towards the formulation of problems and their resolution. The new physical anthropology is marked by the adoption of the genetic level of analysis and the use of *populations,* in the sense of reproductive aggregates, as significant units of reference. (Washburn, 1953). One of the more interesting products of this development has been the involvement of demographers and genticists in the study of particular populations. It has given us studies of Samaritans (Bonné, 1953), Hutterites (Eaton & Mayer, 1953 and Mange, 1964), Dinka (Roberts, 1956), and, more recently, of the people of Tristan da Cunha (Roberts, 1971). Studies of this kind present an invaluable contribution to human ecology.

The concept of population has become a working base for a variety of disciplines including ecology. (Macfadyen, 1963, 87). Although its precise significance is subject to some variation between disciplines, its usage is of considerable convenience for human ecology.

It establishes some brief rapport with another "human ecology"; one which views the community as a symbiotically integrated population and as the effective collective response to environmental influences. (McKenzie, 1934; and Hawley, 1944).

Given a particular population, it becomes possible, as Boughey (1971, 7-8) has pointed out, to demarcate the limits of a trial or exploratory ecosystem which in time may come to constitute the scope of an ecological inquiry. Conversely, we should be able to recognise that, given a particular ecosystem for examination, be it a national park or a city conurbation, the human ecologist's primary task is that of identifying the critical human population.

Man in ordinary circumstances lives his life in company with others. He is a social animal. His relationships with his companions and with the other elements of his habitat find their complete expression at some level of aggregation. These clusterings are defined or established in terms of a wide range of cultural and social criteria. They are not necessarily reproductive isolates. Demographic and bio-physical studies of these human clusters are quick to recognise their need for and dependence upon information regarding cultural and social characteristics. Likewise, ecological studies of human aggregates can expect to make little progress without a very substantial awareness of their socio-cultural attributes. It is at this point that we encounter anthropology's major significance for human ecology.

The human ecologist faces problems unique to him amongst ecologists. His subjects, collections or aggregates of human beings, usually invest themselves and their actions with an assembly of instruments and ideas, collectively known as their culture. They do this in a manner and to a degree without parallel in the animal world. Thus equipped, any human population exists in a total environment which is partly of its own contrivance. This secondary or cultural milieu adds an extra ingredient to the complex of items making up the total environment. The situation is made even more involved for the ecologist in that there is no one uniform human culture. Man is culturally, if not physically, differentiated. It follows then that the human ecological study must possess, as part of its equipment, the means of acquiring an adequate understanding of the cultures it is likely to encounter.

There exist at the moment few more illuminating examples of the practice of human ecology and of its dependence upon an acquaintance with culture and social organization than Sir Frank Fraser Darling's Survey (1955) of the western highlands and islands of Scotland.

The problem presented to the survey was that of "a very old and in many ways primitive human culture existing in an administratively awkward and physically refractory terrain set on the fringe of a highly industrialised urban civilization". (Fraser Darling, 1951). The survey was required to examine the problem and to provide the factual basis for a future policy for the region. The task was undertaken as an exercise in human ecology which in 1944 was "a still uncommon standpoint". (Fraser Darling, 1955, vii). It saw its work as a study of the "interaction of human behaviour, ideas and practices, of the growth and decline of population and their consequences on the terrain and the present generation of folk". (ibid, viii). Two further principles were recognised at the outset. The environment of the critical population, in this case some 120,000 people, would include representatives of another and external human aggregate. The "present" of the inquiry is but a fleeting moment in a continuing process and so the relevant events of the past must be viewed as potentially contributing factors.

When we examine the content of the survey, the dependence upon the specialised interests of anthropology is overwhelmingly apparent. An initial account of the non-human aspect of the problem is followed immediately by a comprehensive, ecologically oriented, demographic survey and analysis. The treatment of the socio-cultural situation gives an indication of the range of factors involved and shown to be relevant. In addition to such obvious topics as land use and tenure, agricultural practice and subsistence economy, the survey looks at the social organization of settlement, the range and nature of voluntary groups and the extent of co-operative activities. Governmental and religious institutions are considered in their relation to other pertinent factors. The relation shown to exist between various religious 'rules of life' and development of community interaction deserves particular mention at the present time. (Fraser Darling, 1955, 315-6).

If example is insufficient to demonstrate the support which anthropology can supply to human ecology, then the survey makes a direct appeal to anthropologists to extend their work amongst the more complex societies. (*ibid,* 281). Happily we can acknowledge that anthropologists have not neglected the challenge to extend their studies beyond the range of the "primitive" world. Thus, for example, we have a small but continually growing collection of studies of European communities. One such, which is not only an anthropological study but provides also much of the additional environmental data required by the ecologist, relates to the parish of Kinvarra, County Galway. (Cresswell, 1969).

Conclusion

Human ecology is that approach which accepts that human aggregates and their total environment are intimately interwoven. Its implicit premise is that populations strive to exist and to maintain themselves in environmental circumstances which are themselves ever-changing to some degree. The resultant actions and interactions, the successes and failures present the ecologist with his subject matter.

In some instances there is every suggestion that a population has successfully solved the problem of survival. It is not necessary to assume that this viability is achieved in consequence of some "perfect fit", of having by luck or judgement arrived at the correct ecological prescription. The ecologist is required, instead, to discover at what cost or inconvenience a population achieves and maintains this happy condition. The implicit acceptance or tolerance of a low level of nutrition, or of a limited degree of ill-health or even the adoption of a practice such as infanticide may be found to be concomitant conditions of group survival. (Weiner, 1964, 503). The obverse strategy is equally possible. Survival in any long term sense may be required to take second place to the insistence upon more highly rated values such as ease of living or longevity. In other words, anthropology may help human ecology to be mindful that it is dealing, not with natural automata but with culturally wilful men.

The human ecologist is confronted with yet another difficulty not shared by other ecologists. He has somehow to minimise the possible errors associated with studying one's own kind. He has to strive after a kind of ecological neutrality. It is still fashionable to present the history of human technology and know-how as evidence of man's inherent ability to dominate his environment. Its accumulative and progressive development is seen as the natural evolution of some specific skill. Economies and ways of life, particularly in their material aspects, are graded to suggest that the "primitive" is necessarily something to be developed and encouraged to become more "advanced". If such "progress" can be shown to have occurred, it is not infrequently because someone has contrived it so and because circumstances have made it possible. Anthropology, generally speaking, can often help in distinguishing between the sequences of history and genuinely evolutionary trends. It can help further by allowing us to see that policies of development, enlightened or exploitative, are themselves factors in a given environment complex. They are, as such, the raw materials of ecological study rather than ecological solutions.

Anthropology shares with human ecology, as some see it at least, the aim of contributing to the natural history of man. Its task is that of describing and understanding the human condition. Both disciplines are concerned with exploration and fact-finding, with research and the development of ideas. Their role in relation to such activities as resource management or exploitation or conservation is that of providing the factual basis of action. To say this is not in any way to minimise the need to conserve or safeguard the conditions upon which we all depend. Population control, conservation of resources and the elimination of unnecessary waste are all urgent requirements at the present time. Their successful achievement is vitally important. Nevertheless, we must be aware of the limitations of human ecology. It can examine and explore particular problem situations in respect of particular individual populations. It can reveal the complexity of factors involved and so expose the nature of the technical task of producing some desired change. It can suggest the kind of plan which would serve the interest of a particular habitat and its particular human occupants. But it can do nothing to ensure that such plans will be acceptable either to the population most directly concerned or to such other populations having an interest in the habitat and its resources. Decisions regarding the adoption of ecologically determined programmes are essentially political decisions. When those decisions are taken and schemes put into operation, the ecologist requires to be on hand to record this intervention and to observe its consequences, both for particular human groups and for the environment at large.

References
Bates, M. (1953) Human Ecology, *Anthropology Today,* A. L. Kroeber (ed.), 700-13, University of Chicago Press, Chicago.

Bews, J. W. (1935) *Human Ecology,* O.U.P., London.

Bonné, B. (1953) The Samaritans: a demographic study, *Human Biology* (35), 61-89.

Boughey, A. S. (1971) *Man and the environment: an introduction to Human Ecology and Evolution,* Collier-Macmillan Ltd, London.

Cresswell, R. (1960) *Une communauté rurale de l'Irlande,* Institut d'Ethnologie, Musée de l'Homme, Paris.

Eaton, J. W. & A. J. Mayer (1953) The social biology of very high fertility among the Hutterites: the demography of a unique population, *Human Biology* (25), 206-64.

Elton, C. (1927) *Animal Ecology,* London.

Forde, C. D. (1948) The integration of anthropological studies, *J. R. Anthrop. Inst.,* LXXVIII, 1-10.

Fraser Darling, F. (1951) The Ecological approach to the social sciences, *American Scientist* (39), 244-54.

Fraser Darling, F. (1953) Man, Caribou and Lichen, *The Listener,* 5th November, 767-9.

Fraser Darling, F. (ed.) (1955) *West Highland Survey: an essay in human ecology,* O.U.P., London.

Gibbs, J. P. & W. T. Martin (1959) Toward a theoretical system of human ecology, *Pacific Sociological Review* 2 (i), 29-36.

Harrison, G. A. (1967) The biological structure of human populations, *Proc. R. Anthrop. Inst.,* 29-36.

Harrison, G. A., J. S. Weiner, J. M. Tanner & N. A. Barnicot (1964) *Human Biology,* Clarendon Press, Oxford.

Hawley, A. H. (1944) Ecology and Human Ecology, *Social Forces* (22), 398-405.

Huntington, C. C. & F. A. Carlsen (1929) *Environmental basis of Social Geography,* New York.

Macfadyen, A. (1963) *Animal Ecology: aims and methods,* 2nd edition, Pitman, London.

McKenzie, R. D. (1934) The field and problems of Demography, Human Geography and Human Ecology, in *The Field and Methods of Sociology,* L. L. Bernard (ed.), 52-66, New York.

Mange, A. P. (1964) Growth and inbreeding of a human isolate, *Human Biology* (30), 114-33.

Quin, J. A. (1940) Topical summary of current literature on human ecology, *American Journal of Sociology,* XLVI, 191-226.

Roberts, D. F. (1956) A demographic study of a Dinka village, *Human Biology* (28), 323-49.

Roberts, D. F. (1971) The Demography of Tristan da Cunha, *Population Studies* (25), 465-79.

Washburn, S. L. (1953) The strategy of Physical Anthropology, *Anthropology Today,* A. L. Kroeber (ed.), 714-27, University of Chicago Press, Chicago.

Weiner, J. S. (1964) *Human Biology,* by Harrison, G. A., J. S. Weiner, J. M. Tanner and N. A. Barnicot; Clarendon Press, Oxford.

Discussion

H. Bowen-Jones. Professor Sheddick has suggested that the human ecologist must be free from the constraints of a single discipline. Can we foresee the eventual establishment of a discipline of human ecology?
V. G. Sheddick. I would suggest that human ecology is not a discipline as such but more an attitude of mind in which one is prepared to recognise that the solving of a problem may require a contribution from a number of specialisms.

8

The Role of Architecture, Planning and Landscape Architecture

M. LLOYD

Traditionally the design professions have accepted several most inhibiting factors in their work. Until the various experiments in advocacy action, convention required the designer to await the approach of his client. This convention has usually restricted the designer's role, methods and type of solution to a problem. The client normally expects the designer to conform to his preconception of that profession's role (for example that an architect will produce a building) and the client has often taken prior decisions which further and critically restrict the type of solution even within the limited sphere defined by his preconception (for example a traffic planner is told that a ring road is required). However within these limits the client expects the designer to solve his problem for him and if he approves of the proposed solution would usually expect the designer to supervise the action necessary to implement the solution. Thus a designer's primary role is one of problem solving but it also has executive and management aspects. Designers are sometimes criticised for not going beyond the conventional limits or for not acting in an anticipatory manner, especially where social or ecological factors would suggest that the conventional solution is not the best. This is discussed, sometimes rather half heartedly, during education. In practice it is a matter of nice judgement and, if one is working within existing conventions, difficult to carry through unless the designer has quite unusual standing, such as architects have had for a generation in Finland.

The professions of architecture, planning and landscape architecture are all concerned with the relationship between man and his environment, but their work is especially aimed at manipulating the environment within fairly well defined limits. Regrettably there has been very little testing of the results of the changes brought about in the environment or of man's reaction to them. Like doctors we can claim that our patients tend to survive and that our work must therefore be satisfactory. Not surprisingly a degree of doubt has arisen in the post-war period when the nature and the scale of the changes being introduced to the social structure and to the physical environment have gone far beyond traditional practice. Not only do these professions have to be sensitive to the psychological, physiological and social reactions of people to the results of their work, they have to attempt to anticipate these reactions when the design only exists as a concept.

Others have done more thorough and precise work on special physiological and psychological requirements, such as NASA on the reactions and needs of a man enclosed in a space capsule. In such a situation the lack of precise information on which to base a design would be catastrophic therefore the willingness to expend research effort, but the routine work of the architect deals with situations which because they lie within or close to normal experience only produce discomfort or dissatisfaction when there is an information or design failure. It is a very rare client that is willing to sponsor research in order to lessen his risk of discomfort. However since the war there has been a great improvement in knowledge of the performance of building fabrics as a modifier of the physical environment, and this has been accompanied by parallel improvements in knowledge of human comfort levels and physiological performance. There has been some improvement in the psychological field but in the main this is still the area of aesthetic judgement where matters of shape, colour, texture and even the ability to orientate oneself is concerned. That this often results in failure is demonstrated by the airport lounge syndrome symptom of a non-space organised by electronic signposts and disembodied voices. Sociological information of a type which assists planners and architects to test their ideas predictively is still very thin. Partly this results from the great disparity of attitudes between designers and sociologists and the frustrated hopes that designers, perhaps quite incorrectly, pinned on sociology in the post-war period. Planners are improving their ability to make models of behaviour at the urban scale but a study of the New Towns will show that the models are somewhat imprecise and are subservient to changes in planning fashions.

Having been somewhat disparaging about the amount of reliable theory and information currently available to physical designers in those areas of most interest to ecologists, there is no doubt that the practice of planning, architecture and landscape architecture contains a very large and important body of experience of the relationship between man and his physical environment. This experience should be of vital concern to an emerging discipline of human ecology. When the ecologists come to make use of it they will find themselves faced with a task of turning material, often vague and diffuse, into something reasonably precise and ideally of predictive use. Much of the material has been remarkably resistant so far to this type of examination.

The area which I believe would have particular interest for human ecologists lies in the transition zone between planning and architecture, such as the design of new communities and their environment or the results of changes in physical structures on the social patterns of an existing community. Designers in this type of problem have to work with and across many disciplines. They are expected to achieve desired social and economic goals as a result of the changes they bring about. In their attempt to do so they have to handle information and briefs from many sources often incompatible in form and value system. Thus not only the problem area should be of interest but the skill and techniques of planners as well.

In the post-war period a number of activities with acute ecological implications have been handled by the professions of architecture, planning and landscape architecture. They are not new in themselves nor in involving these professions but the frequency of their occurrence and the degree of professional awareness have increased markedly. Possibly the most important area concerns the movement of people to new places and conditions of living, and can be subdivided into rural resettlement and the process of urbanisation. It is true that both these processes in their most widespread and marked form are found primarily in the developing countries but related phenomena can be observed in the industrialised countries. The creation of 'New Towns' in Britain being a most interesting varient on both and one where the designers come closest to having a clean slate at the outset.

Although the problems of rural resettlement and of urbanisation are far from the normal experience of the design professions, these professions have played a leading part in trying to come to terms with these processes. Because of the serious nature of these processes, where failure can be catastrophic, because of the exceptionally wide range of disciplines which have to be intimately interwoven I suggest that people with a background of these types of experience have potentially a particularly valuable contribution to make to any human ecological study. It has certainly been my experience that the demands these processes make have succeeded in breaking down disciplinary barriers and inhibitions and welding disparate people together into an effective team in a way which no normal professional co-operation could ever do.

Although it may not be immediately apparent designers, especially architects, deal with very complex requirements in the problems they attempt to solve. Design is a process of optimisation and by definition is the resolving of competing, often conflicting demands. The numbers of variables normally handled simultaneously during the design process is large. There are also many requirements which have to be satisfied in the solution often for a number of 'clients' who may be only partially recognised as such. Ideally architects and planners try to solve a number of problems simultaneously, whilst engineers tend to be concerned with one overriding problem in their design work. For example, in his normal working situation the structural engineer is concerned to achieve stability and safety in a structure to withstand predicted loadings within a cost limit and a range of materials and construction techniques. To help him achieve this he has fairly well developed scientific, technical and mathematical tools, even so value judgements are involved. If one compares this to the architect's problem there is a wealth of practice but only recently any precise techniques. Even in a straight-forward building he is trying to incorporate all the engineer's concerns but together with the provision of space of the appropriate kind for a variety of functions in an optimum relationship, give the parts and the whole an appearance not only to fulfill the basic requirements of psychological well being but also to invest them with symbolic values, the whole to function satisfactorily physiologically, climatically and economically. Unfortunately the client often cannot give precise predictions of the use and changes the requirements during the design process, but none the less expects results of quality. Hospital design is amongst the most difficult at the present but illustrates the general development in the kinds of problem now confronting designers. The 'client' can no longer be easily identified but has become a number of bodies and people, the medical profession, the patients, the visiting public, the Ministry who themselves represent several conflicting client concerns. The buildings are highly complex needing very divergent but technically extreme and precise conditions to be maintained. Most difficult of all is that medical practice is changing at a faster rate than the design process can create solutions. The responses to this rapid change in use all require that the building be looked upon as maleable and no longer as monumental. Very similar developments are taking place in both educational and industrial building programmes. This means that the public as well as the professions have to change their attitudes towards artifacts and buildings from a static to a dynamic one. As a result designers have already found it necessary to revise their methods of work and strengthen their technical skills. The design professions also have to carry out an executive and managerial role. This applies to a lesser extent to planners, but for architects this can be a major part of their work. There is therefore experience in taking part in a team to implement a solution and often being held responsible for the leadership of the team. Today with the complexity of the problems facing the designers, the team tends to emerge at an early stage of the design process and no longer only on site. This type of team work is the normal context of design for planners. The team may be composed of different disciplines and different executive levels. Due to many causes, not least education, there is a lack of common language and often a jockeying for position within the team. However the understanding of team work both to solve problems and to carry out tasks is improving, there is certainly plenty of experience to draw on and this is being studied. The importance of efficient management lead the architectural profession in this country to revise its techniques in a rather thorough manner about ten years ago. It quickly became apparent that many management techniques were to do with problem solving so that the interaction has been particularly fruitful. This increased emphasis on management has given practice, but to an even greater extent education a more operational attitude. Although design for architects, planners and landscape architects has always been a process of problem solving, it had operated within fairly well defined limits and relied on practice and intuition. Design meant concern for the form and style of an object, and in the latin languages that is still its meaning. However architecture increasingly concerned itself with a wider range of problems and the distinct branches of planning and industrial design were already apparent in the inter-war period. Even where style was still appropriate it was rejected as an historical application and it was sought to make objects or buildings appear "functional". Having gone through a philosophical rejection of style and having experienced design as applied to a variety of situations, it was not a long step to redefining design completely as the process of solving problems. The limits and the reliance on 'good practice' and intuition have thus become increasingly untenable during this century, but it is only in the last decade that design method as such has emerged. It was realized that the processes of problem solving were probably generalised but hidden by the differences in languages of the different disciplines. This was amply confirmed by the Imperial College conference of 1962. However, architects having once realised the potential have continued to collect and refine promising techniques as well as develop new techniques themselves. The discovery that there was a fund of experience and techniques available in disciplines normally outside that covered by the visual arts confirmed the new attitude in the minds of many architects and has had profound effects on architectural education. Recently an intermingling has taken place in much of architectural education between design method and management studies. One of the most immediate results has been the change of emphasis which had been implied and latent in much architectural work and thought of the last hundred years. In the present context it also has most important implications for the emerging field of ecology, that is if the people engaged in this discipline are not going to restrict themselves to becoming descriptive scientists but are, as society is demanding, going to attempt to solve any of the critical situations facing us today.

I am not proposing that ecologists become exclusively problem orientated as I am too well aware of the gaps in knowledge and understanding. I do believe however that a large proportion must become professionally problem oriented if present alarms are to be tackled by properly equipped people. To continue to deny action by the repeated call for more knowledge or to take up the extreme preservationist stand within the conservation movement will surely guarantee that someone else, probably less equipped, will attempt the problem and that with public expectations so high the lack of fulfilment would create an atmosphere of rejection.

I have already hinted at the great difficulty designers face due to inadequate information and theory. This was not too crippling when designers worked within the limits of practice, and the demands were less specialised and the rate of change was far slower. Now designers face problems never confronted before, whose rate of change and development are unpredictable, such as the South Hampshire Planning Study. This proposed a method of grasping the problems of creating a conurbation of three million with unknown rates of growth. The difficulty here was that the method started to use a type of language arising out of computer logic and mathematics whilst the public and the design professions are educated to be able to understand a literary and a visual presentation. The South Hampshire Study was a pioneer but in general society has demanded solutions to problems of increasing complexity and has required that these be carried out to higher levels of technical precision. This has also been a period when construction techniques and materials have proliferated. In some areas, primarily those relating to engineering or physics, rather precise theories and information are available but in others instinct, intuition and commonsense have to be relied upon. There is often a gap in the understanding of the research worker as to the designer's needs in terms of the type of information, the manner of its presentation and the degree of precision that he requires. The physical environment is a paradoxical area of work, an elegant solution can arise out of imprecise information that has been handled with fine judgement. People use their surroundings in a broad way, that being so they have not required their buildings to be finely tuned instruments. Even so the information upon which a designer is asked to act is often vague in the extreme. This has to be rectified as far as possible but only allows him to avoid action in exceptional circumstances. Similarly the techniques for predicting the impact of the solution are often very rudimentary, particularly the effects on behaviour and social structure. The designer has always had to act with incomplete and imperfect theory and information, he has deplored it but has had to learn to live with it. This problem of information would appear to be closely analogous to the present and foreseeable future of ecology. That designers are used to solving problems under such conditions and have done so with a modest degree of success is a skill that could be perhaps a valuable contribution that they can make to ecologists.

Architectural education has clearly been effective in forming the attitudes and skills which enable architects to operate. It has made architects problem oriented, but in such a way that they seek all the problems that they think may be associated with the one they first had presented to them, then they try to integrate the solution to all these into a coherent whole, and all the while with a very uncertain state of information.

In my experience design is learnt by doing, and this process has to start at once in higher education. It is true that a small number of exceptional people have developed this type of ability during their professional life but it is an extremely difficult and time wasting way to gain these skills. Secondary education is still primarily based on learning facts with some analytical experience and only very recently and only to a small extent concerned with synthesis. Thus the difficulties of higher education are relatively light when it is desired to direct the student towards an absorption with a discipline and a research pursuit. The difficulties are of quite another magnitude when the student is to be directed towards an integrative activity calling on many disciplines and where creative thought is called for in resolving or optimising apparent conflicting requirements. I believe that those who are going to attempt to lessen the gaps in our knowledge should also, at least as students, experience the difficulties of problem solving for the reasons I have mentioned above. I must re-emphasise that it is my experience that design ability can be learnt but that this is achieved by doing design. If such experience is delayed until a thorough grounding in a discipline is gained then it is difficult, even unlikely that the student will develop design ability. Hence the difficulties that have been encountered by some schools of architecture when they have increased to a marked extent the discipline basis in their curriculum and the difficulties usually encountered in post-graduate planning studies.

All this apart, as Professor Christopher Jones has said it is necessary to create understanding across disciplines, which although he was talking about design must surely apply to ecology, and as he has said it is better to create understanding within people by design experience where many disciplines of both arts and sciences have to be combined rather than try to create links later between disciplines. Interdisciplinary teams will still be necessary but are likely to function more effectively and gain in creative insights when the members already have the flexibility of mind and a mutual understanding from their education. Such an experience during education may also go some little way towards the creation of a common language which is seriously lacking today. This has been my experience in a university in Africa where architects, planners, engineers and social scientists joined together in design work.

Twenty years ago design education was based on an odd mixture of Beaux Arts and Bauhaus traditions but it put the problem solving situation (studio work) at the core of the curriculum and teaching method. It was effective at forming attitudes and skill but was seriously lacking in efficient working methods. From the thirties onwards there had been a widening of the disciplinary scope of design education and in the post-war period this continued with particular interest in numeracy, information theory and the social sciences. The project based nature of the teaching was maintained and gradually strengthened, so that from being the basis of the design work, it began to have effects on the teaching of theoretical subjects. A long line of educational experiments and an evolving change of attitude to design itself had prepared the ground. In the sixties design method grew almost explosively, at last tools became available and branches of other disciplines, such as mathematical heuristics, or other techniques, such as systems analysis, became incorporated into design. Now architectural education can offer not only a means to create attitudes and skills but begins to have problem solving tools of some precision. Ecologists may well suggest that whilst this odd form of education may work for designers, in ecology there is an immense field of knowledge which has to be studied. I can assure them that an architect or a planner has also an immense field of knowledge which he has to master, indeed we cannot contain it in five years of study. But as Professor Hinton has pointed out, where schools have increased theoretical and disciplinary study at the expense of design the students have been of less use in practice and in the field.

The dynamic processes of society must continue, and this means change if not 'development' in society and its environment. It is one of the main tasks of ecologists to ensure that as far as possible these changes are beneficial in the long term as well as the short term. The present situation where those concerned with the environment have to continually carry out retrieval and repair jobs is ludicrous and wasteful. The ecologist must take part in the design and control of change in the relationship between man and his environment. There is no doubt that they can learn from those professions which hitherto have had to design and implement change in the environment, but hopefully they will add a great deal more awareness and precision to the process of change which at present is so haphazard. If they accept such a role then it is my belief that their education has to change drastically. So far it is mostly concerned with further study of more disciplines. Too little attention appears to be given to creating the ability to integrate diverse disciplines, attitudes and data into a coherent synthesis, and even less attention in curriculum content or teaching method is given to exercising the student in this activity and more importantly challenging him to apply his skill and knowledge to create solutions to problems. Therefore I particularly emphasize the impact and implications that changes in project based design education have had in the physical design professions. I suggest that design education is the most vital contribution that these professions can make to ecology.

Discussion

P. Walker, Huddersfield Polytechnic. Do you think that it is better for ecologists to be involved in professional training such as that for architects, rather than for ecologists to try to become architects? For example, a particular school of architecture may develop a bias towards ecology, and the architects which it trains would be especially fitted for particular aspects of architecture.

M. Lloyd. I would certainly say that a school of architecture, planning or landscape architecture which did not have a major ecological component would be grossly irresponsible. I am not advocating that ecologists do some part-time architecture or that architects do some part-time ecology but that the design activity undertaken during architectural training is an extremely valuable aspect of that training, and one which could be applied, with benefit, in the education of human ecologists.

M. J. L. Hussey. A difficulty involved in project work of this kind is that any worthwhile problem which is to be considered by students is likely to require knowledge in depth which the student may not have. One therefore has to accept a superficial solution and the student may not be capable of viewing his solutions critically.

M. Lloyd. There is a real danger of getting a superficial answer. On a more general point, one is also likely to end up either with brilliant innovators or appalling dilettantes! One way in which this can be overcome is by involving the student in real problems not synthetic ones. Student involvement will then be very much improved, and, just as important, both students and staff involved will be forced to recognise the degree of their ignorance.

H. Bowen-Jones. If one can take the student into real situations, then I am quite sure that those are the instances where the learning happens.

9

The Contribution of Medical Science
to the Study of Human Ecology

D. R. HANNAY

The origins of medical science can be traced in part to classical Greece, where medicine became formalised as a discipline and a profession. Medical students still take the Hippocratic oath, and Hippocrates described the good physician as one "who has a due regard to the seasons of the year, and the diseases which they produce; to the states of the wind peculiar to each country and the qualities of its waters; who marks carefully the localities of towns, and of the surrounding country, whether they are low or high, hot or cold, wet or dry; who, moreover, takes note of the diet and regimen of the inhabitants, and in a word, of all the causes that may produce disorder in the animal economy". The Hippocratic writings on Airs, Waters, and Places are about the relationship between human beings and their environment, and as such are a treatise on Human Ecology.

In broader terms, all societies whether preliterate or modern have developed means of coping with disease which involve specific healers such as doctors or priests, and treatments which imply a cause. The whole invariably reflects the cosmology of the culture concerned, whether the closed thought systems of primitive religion and magic, the interpretations of theology or the explanations of molecular biology. Man is uniquely self-aware, and his relationship with his environment depends on how he perceives himself and the world around him. This in turn determines the nature of his healers. In primitive societies a witch doctor may be the intermediary for tribal gods and good health. Two hundred years ago the medical examiners in London were the Dean of St. Paul's and the Bishop of London. Today a physician is much more likely to be examined by a biochemist than a priest. What was once a sin is now a sickness, and medicine is increasingly expected to be the arbiter of moral judgments. The application of the scientific method has certainly not decreased the extent to which medicine is culturally defined, but it has tended to fragment medical knowledge. It is therefore worth considering the contribution of the different disciplines of medical science to the study of Human Ecology.

The basic preclinical sciences include Anatomy, Physiology, Bio-chemistry and, increasingly, Behavioural Science. The study of Anatomy has related structure to function and thrown light on the evolution of man. Physical characteristics such as body build can be seen as arising from adaptations to particular environments in the past, and related to modern mechanical design through Ergonomics. Physiology has told us more and more about the homeostatic mechanisms which maintain what Claude Bernard called the *milieux intérieux* of the body in an ever-changing external world. We can assess the range and optimum levels of factors such as noise and nutrition. Poverty was first defined by Seebohm Rowntree at the turn of this century, largely in terms of the money required to buy essential food; an assessment made possible by nutritional studies. Malnutrition is still the world's most common malady, both medical and ecological. At a micro and molecular level, biochemistry enables man to monitor the effects of ingested chemicals, and study the pharmacological action of drugs. Although the one may be unconscious and the other conscious, both are increasingly important in the complex relationship between man and his environment.

Last, but not least, of the basic disciplines are the behavioural sciences, which alone could be counted as a major contribution to the study of Human Ecology. It is not, however, inappropriate to consider them briefly as a basic medical science because the main causes of death and disease in industrial societies are predominantly behavioural in their aetiology and, therefore, prevention. Psychology, Social Anthropology, and Sociology are usually taken to comprise the Behavioural Sciences, and are particularly relevant to both medicine and ecology. The experimental techniques of psychology and the observations of social psychology have told us a great deal about the reactions of individuals and groups to external stimuli and situations. This is important for the study of inter-personal relationships, and occupational health. The insights of Social Anthropology have shown the relativeness of cultural values, including our own concepts of health and medical care. Medical sociology is an expanding field concerned not only with the social aetiology of disease but with the definitions and behaviour of sickness and the nature of the healing professions. The study of behaviour is crucial to understanding how individuals react to their environment and how society adapts to perceived disfunction in itself. The social environment of man is as important as the physical, both for human ecology and for medicine.

Turning to clinical science, pathology is concerned with the body's reactions to hostile conditions. It includes the effect of micro-organisms and chemicals, and covers the study of morbid anatomy. Crude descriptions have given way to the more precise definitions of microscopy, and now a whole range of techniques in biochemistry and cell biology are used to investigate the mechanism of reactions rather than just to classify the changes. Pure description has been augmented by experimental biology, and diseases of specific aetiology have been replaced by conditions whose causes are multi-factorial. The practice of clinical medicine reflects the change of disease prevalence as well as therapeutic advance. It is difficult for us to appreciate today how sanitation, immunization, and antibiotics have completely transformed the spectrum of sickness. One hundred years ago in this country a third of all deaths were due to infectious diseases; today the proportion is less than 1%. As recently as 1941 there were 50,000 cases of diphtheria in England and Wales alone, and 2,400 children died from the disease. Yet few doctors qualified since the war have ever seen a case in this country. The greatest change has been during the first years of life. Infant mortality is now a tenth of what it was in the 19th century, and it is largely this which accounts for the overall increase in life expectancy. But death rates in middle age have not decreased to anything like the same extent, and hardly at all in the elderly. In order to reach three score years and ten in the last century one had to be a great deal tougher than today. Death rates in the middle-aged started to fall at the turn of this century with sanitary reform and a rise in the standard of living. The decline continued until the early 1920's when there was a change and the death rates for middle-aged men, unlike those for women, ceased to fall and have remained almost static since, at twice the level for women.

Infectious diseases in the young have been replaced by new epidemics in the middle-aged, of which the most important is ischaemic heart disease (or coronary thrombosis). This changed pattern of disease experience is part of an alteration in the relationship of man to his environment, and is reflected in many ways. The population structure of industrial countries is no longer a broad based pyramid, but rectangular with an increasing number of elderly. Fever hospitals and sanitoria have given way to intensive care units for the victims of coronary thrombosis, and transplant surgery. The general physician is being replaced by specialists either for systems of the body such as cardiologists, or for age groups such as the paediatrician and, increasingly, the geriatrician. Fifty years ago if a family doctor had done an appendicectomy on the kitchen table it might have been considered heroic, but if he did it today he would more likely be struck off the register. There is nothing immutable about doctors or medicine. The role of the general practitioner is now more concerned with the management of chronic disease, with emotional problems, and with prevention and screening. Or rather it should be, but professions and institutions are slow to adapt. We still link prestige to large hospitals built for posterity, when posterity would be more grateful for something less permanent and preferably not required at all.

Just as personal health is the adaptation of an individual, so public health is the adaptation of society. This adaptation is not so much a blue-print for survival, if you will pardon the expression, but a continual process of change which adjusts the relationship of man to his environment. Success depends on how sensitive we are to changes most of which are directly or indirectly due to man himself. And the rate of change is increasing. The dictates of Galen held sway for centuries, but scientific medicine has brought incredible changes in the past fifty years. The long-standing traditions of religious bodies and charitable institutions are being rapidly replaced by the collective responsibility of the State. Within twenty-five years of the birth of the National Health Service the tripartite structure of that Service will be altered again into integrated area health boards. It is important that these changes are not just accepted as being desirable in themselves, but that we evaluate and monitor the results. This requires the means of information feed-back, and an organisational and political structure which is capable of reacting effectively.

Surgery is perhaps more dependent on technical advances than is clinical medicine, but these advances raise profound questions about human values. It is not possible to practise transplant surgery without reference to cultural ethics, any more than it is to indulge in euthanasia and abortion. Values are an integral part of the way in which men perceive themselves in relation to each other and the world around them. It is not enough to explain the nature of man by saying that he was an ape; it is what we are that matters. Man cannot stand back completely from the study of mankind without denying part of himself. We have to decide, because we can guide the process ourselves.

Science without conscience is but death of the soul, wrote Montaigne, and nowhere is this more true than in medical science. We cannot hide behind our techniques.

The part of medical science most clearly related to human ecology is that of public health, social and preventive medicine, or community medicine. The terms themselves reflect the evolution of concern from the time when the sanitary commission was set up under Edwin Chadwick, and the first medical officer of health appointed to cope with the appalling conditions of 19th century industrial England. Individual patient care was useless unless the environmental causes of disease were remedied, like polluted water supplies and bad housing. The goal of medicine should be prevention as well as cure, and both require the resources and organisation of society as a whole. To be effective these resources must be integrated on a community basis and not split between hospitals, general practice, and local authorities. Modern community medicine is concerned with the epidemiology of disease and the organisation of health and social services. It includes the application of behavioural science both to the aetiology of disease and to the delivery of medical care.

The four main causes of death in industrial countries are cardiovascular disease (coronary thrombosis), cerebrovascular disease (strokes), cancer, and respiratory disease, especially bronchitis. All these conditions are predominantly multifactorial in origin and therefore in prevention, and human behaviour is of major importance in their causation. This behaviour is not at the whim of impersonal epidemics, but involves personal decisions about the way an individual lives. The typical patient with coronary artery disease is a cigarette-smoking middle-aged man who is somewhat overweight and likes his food. Though sedentary he works hard and is successful according to the values of his culture. The sufferer from chronic bronchitis is of similar age and sex, but more likely to be a blue collar worker living in poorer surroundings. There is no single cause for these conditions, which are largely due to individual habits of living, conditioned by contemporary culture. This social environment is just as relevant to health as the physical environment; it is how, as well as where, man lives that matters. There are no specific diseases, wrote Florence Nightingale — there are specific disease conditions.

Many of these conditions are poorly understood. We do not know why people living on some of the Western Isles of Scotland have a higher average blood pressure than control groups in Glasgow who might be expected to be more at risk from the so-called stresses of urban life. It is not known why some cancers appear more prevalent in the Outer Hebrides than on the mainland. Even if a cause is understood there is often little that we can do about it. It is conservatively estimated that cigarette smoking kills about 50,000 people a year in the United Kingdom alone from heart disease, lung cancer, and chronic bronchitis. Lung cancer in men has increased more than fifty-fold during this century, and 90% is caused by the smoking of cigarettes. Atmosphere pollution plays only a very small part; lung cancer rates are high in the Channel Islands where the air is fresh and cigarettes are cheap. In view of the fact that there are infinitely safer ways of indulging in tobacco, the flourishing sales of cigarettes must rank as one of the most astonishing episodes of self-deception and self-destruction in recent history. These modern life-shortening diseases are unlikely to be selected out, because they are mainly degenerative conditions which set in after the reproductive years. It has even been suggested that some chronic diseases may have an adaptive origin. For instance increased insulin might be an advantage for a hunter gatherer who feasts occasionally between long fasts, but could lead to the production of insulin antibodies and diabetes when food becomes abundant. A hunting-food gathering existence has been man's ecological niche for over 99% of his existence on this planet.

If maladaptations of individual behaviour are important causes of death today they are also major sources of disability, from accidents, alcoholism, drug addiction, and mental illness which today accounts for over 40% of the hospital beds in the Western Region of Scotland. It is interesting that the one infectious disease which is on the increase in this country is gonorrhoea, for which the behavioural implications are obvious. Social patterns of ill health involve the complexities of personal relationships as well as habits. "The single patient who is ill by himself is rather the exception", said T. S. Eliot's physician in *The Cocktail Party*. In many ways it is easier to remedy defects in the physical environment than it is in the social setting of disease, which is perhaps encouraging in view of the enormous problems of urban squalor throughout the world. Infant mortality in Glasgow is still higher than in the rest of the U.K., much of the difference being due to appalling housing. This means that in the 1970s thousands of families in Glasgow still live in crowded conditions without basic amenities, where the chance of a baby dying is twice that of the better housed in the same city.

Epidemiology is very much the study of how people adapt to their environment, and the study of medical care provision extends this concept of adaptive response to society as a whole. How are limited resources best utilised to meet a demand which appears to grow as each medical advance opens up fresh horizons of need? How can increasing specialisation be humanised so that the whole person is not forgotten as the end rather than the means of technical excellence? How do we translate an apparently caring community into effective community care, where prevention and long term maintenance of function are seen to be as important as the drama of acute ill health? These are the challenges of community medicine and in essence they are ecological.

The history of public health has been divided, like most things, into three. Firstly, the long period of authority from antiquity to the beginnings of medical science; secondly, the era of research, and treatment of specific diseases; and lastly, the era of ecology when the whole patient and the community rather than the disease entity become the focus of medical attention. It is not for nothing that introductory courses in Human Ecology are being developed for medical students. It may be that such a viewpoint will transform the role of medicine in society. National prestige is still measured in terms of the amount spent on health services and the number of new hospitals, when perhaps the opposite should be the case. Plato asserted in his Republic that the need for many hospitals and doctors was the mark of a bad city. Physicians, according to him, were only of use for the treatment of wounds and during epidemics, and to invent new names for diseases. He considered it abominable "to stand in need of the medical art through sloth and intemperate diet".

The wheels of medicine and ecology seem once more to be running together, but they have not just turned full circle because modern man presses on his environment as never before. Many of the resulting problems may best be tackled by the methodologies of medical science applied from the viewpoint of human ecology. What are the lasting effects of early influences? What are the delayed and indirect results of environmental stimuli and pollutants? What are the effects of a crowding on hormonal activities, on stress, and behavioural patterns? Is there a critical urban mass and can we balance privacy with social interaction? What is the range of man's adaptive potential? But facts alone are not enough; we must have the will to adapt for "Will is stronger than fact — it can mould and overcome fact, but this world has still to discover its will". Nowhere is this more true than of population growth; we know the facts, but have we the will to adapt in time? One of the causes of the population avalanche is the triumph of medical science over specific disease entities, but this will be a pyrrhic victory if malnutrition and overcrowding take their place. Medicine has the means to stabilise population growth, but society has yet to will the end through all the complexities of man's motivation and morality.

It seems appropriate to conclude by adapting the words of one of the founders of modern medicine — the pathologist Rudolf Virchow. He wrote in the last century that "politics is medicine writ large". Today it is Human Ecology which is medicine writ large.

References

Dubos, R. (1965) *Man Adapting,* Yale University Press.

Ewald, W. R. (1967) *Environment for Man,* Indiana University Press.

Kilbourne and Smillie (1969) *Human Ecology and Public Health,* Collier-MacMillan.

Morris, J. N. (1964) *Uses of Epidemiology,* Livingstone Ltd.

Suchman, E. A. (1963) *Sociology and the Field of Public Health,* Russell Sage Foundation.

Discussion

J. Grant. You mentioned the problem of infant mortality rates in Glasgow. Isn't the main problem in Glasgow the high birth rates in the poorer areas, making the provision of new housing a continual and expanding problem?

D. R. Hannay. I was making a rather different point, namely, that during the post neo-natal period, from one month to one year, infant mortality in areas with poor housing conditions is nearly double that in better areas, this being irrespective of size of family. This is an example of environmental conditions being highly relevant to health in this country.

Perhaps I could make one general comment on the nature of human ecology. Should we look on it as a discipline? My feeling is that human ecology is more of a "value perspective" than a distinct discipline.

Part 3
Course Opportunities

10
The A Level
Environmental Studies Syllabus

S. McB. CARSON

The traditional sixth former represented about 7% of a year group. He was in school terms the most successful academic pupil and his aim was to enter a university (with colleges of education for those who failed to get there). In recent years due to the advent of 'comprehensive' education the sixth form has opened its gates to other students. Indeed after some initial opposition many schools have abandoned any qualification barriers to sixth form entry. The sixth form today will include 25% of a year group or more (often much more in the first year). It includes students staying to obtain one or two additional 'O' levels for entry to a college or profession, others aiming at one or two 'A' levels with colleges, university or professions in mind, and many who are not at all clear what they intend to do next, as well as the traditional bright academic whose road is clear before him.

He is entering the sixth form from a different background from that of his predecessor of a few years ago. The whole centre of gravity of the school has shifted as more students are staying at school to 16 (75% — 85% in many schools and soon to be 100%). As a result the weight of school courses has shifted. He is more mature, more independent, less inclined to accept authority, more demanding, more concerned. Before leaving school he may well be a voting citizen, may be married.

There is an unfortunate myth around (and I've heard it from the mouths of the Schools Council representatives who ought to know better) that the sixth former (indeed the fifth former) is only interested in obtaining paper qualifications for the most rewarding job financially that he can obtain.

All my experience leads me to the conclusion that this is less than the truth. Sixth formers want to participate in society, to improve it, and to equip themselves to do so.

What of the society for which he is being prepared?

Today's sixth former will be fifty in AD 2004. He can confidently expect (war permitting) to see the 21st century well on its way. We must be careful to look forward with him in planning his education and not backward to our own youth.

What can he expect? A world where science and technology will be infinitely more powerful in all fields — where this fact alone will revolutionise established habits of living, of communication, leisure, governments, and present an ever present danger of immediate destruction in war — which grows smaller every year as land is used up or polluted — of exploding population (see M.I.T. predictions) double at least by the end of the century — of declining natural resources and energy capacity.

The results of these pressures will affect all social and political considerations — it will change many established judgements. There will inevitably be world-wide famine, disease, probably war as nations and classes struggle for enough to eat.

Already the pressures are upon our sixth former. He is conscious of the moral problems of contraception and abortion, of the increasing poverty of the 'third world'. He is becoming aware of pollution dangers and conservation policies. He sees on his TV screen daily the horrors of modern war.

The important point is that he is aware that these are problems involving him personally. He can no longer take a detached attitude.

How should these considerations affect our educational provision?

The sixth former must know that his courses are relevant to his needs. He is not concerned with the niceties of academic disciplines but with real open-ended situations. He must participate in his own choices at his own level.

The sixth former is anxious to explore, understand and to come to terms with himself, and also to explore, understand and control the world he lives in. 'Environmental Studies' offers courses geared to this situation. Such courses have common grounds though they may vary enormously in what they cover. Generally they divide into: (a) courses concerned with the biophysical environment and man's reaction with it (man-environment); (b) courses concerned with man and society including man in the built environment (man-man). Their common ground is the concern with inter-relationships; with the flow of energy; ecology; systems. They may be local or world wide in concern (spaceship earth). They provide many problems but few answers. They require information, and reasons but finally subjective and even ethical judgements.

For historical reasons more attention has been given to countryside situations (Rural Environment Studies) than to Urban Studies but since the door is open this is bound to change.

Examination syllabuses exist at 'O' level (including 'O(A)') and at 'A' level.

An 'A' level syllabus of Environmental Studies is needed so that the most able students going on to universities may have an opportunity to consider in depth these environmental problems.

To be accepted a proposed 'A' level syllabus has to pass through a set procedure, that is it must be accepted by an examination board and passed on by them for recognition by the Schools Council. At any stage it may be referred back and the proposers may have to start again. In preparing the Hertfordshire syllabus we were aware of this as we had twice had proposals from one of our schools refused. So we set about this task systematically.

There are certain criteria an 'A' level syllabus must fulfil —
- (a) It must be recognised by a number of university faculties as a qualification for entry.
- (b) It must be generally recognised by universities as indicating the intellectual quality of students.
- (c) It must offer entry to careers at non-graduate level.
- (d) It must offer a unified study relevant to students' needs.
- (e) It must develop its own education methodology.
- (f) It must be a practical proposition in school.

The syllabus has clear objectives —
- (a) To make clear the concept of the ecological inter-relationship of the physical and biological factors that make up the environment.
- (b) To develop skills and attitudes necessary to appreciate the place of Man in the environment and the impact of human society on his biophysical surroundings.
- (c) To study the ways in which Man may control his environmental impact and to recognise the values by which such controls may be guided.

An outline of the syllabus accompanies this paper. The main divisions are — the processes and systems of the natural environment and the limits of the resources base; the ecosystem; the interaction of Man and his environment; environmental conflicts and planning — a field study.

Facilities — teaching and timetabling. Should (or could) this syllabus be taught by a single teacher or by a team? There are arguments for both points of view but a small team would have many advantages. A timetable has been suggested for two teachers sharing the course. In-service training will be required in any case in a number of fields. This needs careful thought. We are providing teachers' courses at appropriate levels in physics for the non-physicist; field studies; planning.

Resources and equipment — these are expensive, a good library is essential. A central resource provision seems an economic possibility.

BRIEF OUTLINE OF 'A' LEVEL SYLLABUS FOR
ENVIRONMENTAL STUDIES

Section One: Processes and Systems of the Natural Environment and the
Limits of the Resources Base

1.1   *The Solar System*

    1.1.1.   Sun as a Source of Energy

    1.1.2.   The Transport of Energy

1.2   *The Atmosphere and Hydrosphere*

    1.2.1.   Atmospheric layers and filtering effects

    1.2.2.   Insolation

    1.2.3.   Weather systems, air masses and climate

    1.2.4.   Water cycle

1.3   *The Lithosphere*

    1.3.1.   The soil

1.4   *The Biosphere*

    1.4.1.   Conception of the circulation of elements

    1.4.2.   Methods of obtaining energy

Section Two: The Ecosystem

The student will carry out an ecological study in the field in connection
with this section to illustrate the theme of energy flow, through the
following topics:

2.1   *Climatic and Edaphic Factors*

2.2   *Pyramids of Numbers*

2.3   *Food Webs*

2.4   *Ecology of Population*

2.5   *Population, Control Mechanisms*

2.6   *Ecology of Communities*

Section Three: The Interaction of Man and the Environment

3.1   *Man as a Heterotrophic Organism*

    3.1.1.   The satisfaction of his fundamental requirements (food,
oxygen, warmth, shelter)

3.2   *The Evolution of Modern Man as a Tool-using, Rational Creature*

    3.2.1.   A consideration of hunter, pastoral and agricultural
societies

    3.2.2.   Man's domestication of plants and animals

    3.2.3.   Man's use of mineral Resources

    3.2.4.   Man's acquisition of energy exploiting techniques and
their application to his evolutionary success

3.3   *Pressures on the Environment*

    3.3.1.   Reproductive capacity and population explosion in
underdeveloped countries

    3.3.2.   The industrial revolution

    3.3.3.   Effects on the environment of urbanization

    3.3.4.   Mechanization and intensification of agriculture

    3.3.5.   Further illustrations of pressures on the environment
resulting in degradation

Section Four: Environmental Conflicts and Planning: A Field Study
The student will be expected to select one topic from the list shown at
the end of this section and submit it to the Board for agreement at an
early stage of the course.
The study will be concerned with the interaction of man and the natural
or built environment, i.e.

(a) the influence of man's social and economic activities on
land use, natural resources, townscape and buildings, and on
the balance of living things in the ecosystem;
(b) the effect of change in the natural environment and the
ecosystem on man's activities.

In this section the student will be expected to draw on material from all
previous sections. The headings listed below *are to be regarded as a
check list and should be brought into the study only where relevant to
its objectives.*
The emphasis should be on the inter-relationship of processes and
activities outlined in the syllabus and the internal details only in so far
as they affect these inter-relationships.
The student will be expected to find evidence for himself and to come
to a judgement on the environmental pressures involved in the situation
being studied.
The study will also be a test of the student's familiarity with the
techniques of analysis and evaluation, his grasp of content, handling of
sources, ability in communication and presentation.

4.1 *The Enterprise*
    4.1.1. Identification
    4.1.2. Historical development
    4.1.3. Management and its aims
    4.1.4. External influences
    4.1.5. Resources base
4.2 *Associated Needs*
    4.2.1. Housing and special facilities
    4.2.2. Infrastructure
4.3 *Identification of Environmental Effects*
4.4 *Evaluation and Planning*
    4.4.1. Evaluation of impacts
    4.4.2. Planning

11

The Biology of Man and his Environment at The University of Aston in Birmingham

A. J. MATTY

Elsewhere at this Conference it has been said that human ecology is a "value perspective" rather than a discipline and it would seem that in spite of attempts to define what is meant by human ecology in terms of biological, mathematical and physical scientific parameters the subject is not amenable to discipline categorisation.

The basing of any tertiary education programme on a diffuse foundation does not appear to be sound, and possibly the most worthwhile contribution to the education of human ecologists is the development of a widely ranging course of study grounded in a natural division of science or technology such as the earth sciences, biology or geography or in social sciences, or perhaps even architecture. It may be that in assessing the ecology of man in his natural and created environment more can be learnt and more can be taught by this approach than by adopting an omnibus approach. Also it would indeed be a great pity if human ecology was to be seen going the way of management study, where the art of business management is now rapidly acquiring mystique and pseudo-science.

In the Department of Biological Sciences at the University of Aston in Birmingham, biology related to the ecology of man has been taught for the past five years. In this department it has been the general view that not all but many of the answers to world environmental problems are to be found in a better understanding of the biology of man and his environment. Education in biology for human ecologists is, it is felt, of paramount importance, but not in any sense of Victorian social Darwinism.

The development of the course entitled "The Biology of Man and his Environment" has been somewhat pragmatic and very much concerned as one might expect in a technological university, with immediate applicability of biology in the social environment. The course is limited solely to the consideration of biology, for here one must agree with Professor Bowen-Jones who has said that any course in higher education claiming to be concerned centrally with the inter-relationship of man and the environment must either be honestly described as having certain limitations of coverage or be defensible in terms of comprehensive balance. The limitation of coverage of this course is to biology. The Biology of Man and his Environment has been taught as a three-year course in the Combined Honours degree at Aston for the past five years. This degree is a three-subject first year and a two-subject second and third year type of degree and subjects as diverse as French and ergonomics may be taken in the final two years. The Biology of Man and his Environment is normally read with a science subject such as chemistry or geology, although there are numerous exceptions to this rule. For example, there are students reading French with Biology of Man and combinations such as education and economics with Biology of Man are also encouraged.

The course was initially conceived because the Biological Sciences B.Sc. degree at Aston demanded A-level chemistry, was directed to experimental, quantitative biology and contained very little content of "Human Biology". However, as the Department of Biological Sciences contained active research groups in applied hydrobiology, biodeterioration, applied microbiology and biomedical science, it was decided to utilise this expertise, along with that of others to teach "those aspects of biology which help us to understand *Homo sapiens,* his societies and his environment" (Senate definition of the course). It was found that the members of staff of the Department knew something about the biology of man; they knew something about certain aspects of the biology of the environment but there was no teaching of human ecology.

The course was designed initially to cover material which was of interest to a majority of students, not only those inclined to become professional biologists; to fit students to teach in (as we thought then, five years ago) post-Dainton secondary schools and to concentrate on the biology and ecology of a single species, thus giving a concentration and coherence which could be lacking in a more diverse syllabus of conventional biology taken as half of a Combined Honours degree.

Regarding the content of the course. Firstly, since there is a qualifying examination after the end of the first year, Part I had to be an entity in itself, for some students elect to drop the course after one year. A necessary A-level for entry to the course at the moment is biology. The first year is a deepening and widening of A-level, for it has been found that A-level biology students generally have had very little teaching of certain aspects of the physiology of man, such as the cardio-vascular system, the respiratory system, the urinary system and the skin and control of body temperature. These aspects are outlined. However, it is biochemistry, genetics and microbiology that form the core of the year. A knowledge of the elements of biochemistry is felt to be basic, not only to an understanding of human physiology but also to many biological industries, to certain aspects of genetics and microbiology and to several methods of controlling the biological environment. The introductory course of biochemistry deals first with the composition, nomenclature and properties of basic biochemistry and then shows how these substances interact in a dynamic fashion in cellular metabolism.

Genetics, most biologists are insistent, is essential to any study of the biology of man and his environment, and although genetics is taught in the first year of this course, it is also carried through into the second and third years.

In the first year the introductory course on cytogenetics consists of, to quote the syllabus: "the physical basis of inheritance. Life cycles: sexual and asexual reproduction. Mendelian principles. Independent assortment and genetic recombination. Chromosome mapping. The basis of variation: gene mutation. Chromosomal mutation. Maternal effects and cytoplasmic heredity. Quantitative inheritance in man, polygenes. Inborn errors of metabolism. Introduction to population genetics".

Thirdly, microbiology and its importance for a full understanding of the biology of human ecology cannot be overstated. Hence the introductory course in microbiology consists of: an introductory survey of the main groups of micro-organisms; bacterial, fungi and algae and protozoa. The beneficial and detrimental activities of micro-organisms and their industrial use. The causation of disease in man, animals and plants; the spoilage of man's food and environment and the control of micro-organisms by disinfection, sterilization and antibiotics are also studied.

In addition, in this first year, time is devoted to introducing some of the invertebrate animals which are competing for parts of the same environmental niche as man.

Finally, development is discussed both in man and animals; many of the patterns seen in development are those of adaptations to the environment. Embryology may not be as "trendy" as molecular biology today, but some understanding of its principles might serve well the training of human ecologists — "ex ovo omnia".

It will be noticed that the first year contains no animal and plant ecology; this is not an ecology course, although in the second year there is an introduction to the concepts of ecology which includes some definitions in ecology.

In the second year we introduce further subjects which are thought to be important to the understanding of the biology of man and his environment. One of these is an introduction to virology and immunology for viruses certainly are one of our greatest biological environmental hazards. Also, radiobiology is introduced in the second year because with the ever-increasing use and mis-use of radio-isotopes and ionising radiations by man, a knowledge of their effects on biological systems becomes increasingly important. It is also useful to know something of the more hazardous isotopes present in man's environment. With this object in mind the course then covers such topics as nature of the hazard from ionising radiation, measurement of ionising radiation and the action on living systems, radiation in the environment and isotopes and food chains.

Genetics is continued in the second year, this time human cytogenetics. Again from the syllabus: "The human karyotype. The Lyon hypothesis, mosaicism, chromosomes in cancer, sex determination, sex ratio, intersexual states. Genes, enzymes and errors of metabolism. Genes in populations. Human variability. Anthropometry, photogrammetry, somatotyping".

Statistics and the origin and evolution of man are also taught in the second year.

In the third year genetics is further discussed, this time with the emphasis more on human social biology, twin studies, psychogenetics, medical genetics and, inevitably, genetic aspects of race. The works of Jensen, Eysenck and Bodmer are compulsory reading here! Also in the third year, neurophysiology and behaviour are given a large share of the course. Here, in addition to the necessary descriptive neurosensory physiology, primate ethology and human behaviour teaching play a major part; drive and conflict behaviour, the evolution of behaviour, relationship between learning and instinct are among the topics introduced to the students.

Although a short course in human nutrition is given in the third year, the remainder of the year is devoted to teaching aspects of environmental biology which stem from the research activities of the department. Firstly, in discussing the effects of human societies on ecological systems, water pollution and water management is studied. This is because the department has a section of applied hydrobiology which runs an M.Sc. course in "The Biology of Water Management". Secondly, problems of biodeterioration and biodegradation are discussed because again, in the department there is a Biodeterioration Information Centre which provides practical research, information and industrial liaison in the fields of biodeterioration and biodegradation. Biodeterioration is concerned with ways of controlling the environment to prevent the attack of living organisms on materials. Biodegradation is the process by which materials — usually waste products — are broken down biologically. From this stems the teaching of the principles and ecological aspects of biodeterioration including the study of specific groups of deteriogens; wood, food and engineering biodeterioration, along with methods of control.

Thirdly, as there is a section of the department dealing with industrial biochemical fermentation, particularly with the production of single cell protein, this is also taught.

Finally, students are expected to carry out in their third year an extended exercise on some aspect of their course work. This exercise may take the form of a critical evaluation of a particular subject, or may be of an experimental nature.

Although at the moment the course does not include hormonal influences or behaviour, perhaps in the future any *man and his environment* course should include teaching something about how hormones are essential to our understanding of behavioural patterns. Already the effects of hormones and stress and the effects of over-crowding of mice on hormonal balance are well known and the subject of pheromones, that is chemicals which act as sexual and behavioural attractants at a distance, is now being actively studied in primates and man, and maybe it is a much more important subject in our behavioural inter-relationships and with the environment than we think.

This course, as outlined above, tries to bring together certain aspects of the biology of man, his genetics, his physiology, his nutrition and his susceptibility to disease and to place them alongside certain biological conditions of the environment.

The growth of student numbers on the course has been rapid and in the last four years the *entry* has risen from 30 to 60. In fact 60 students has been set as the upper limit due to space restrictions. Also the number of students entering the second year of the course, i.e. students who after passing the first part of the examination have opted to continue with Biology of Man and his Environment, has increased from 36% to 84%. Thus the course would appear to be popular with students.

An analysis of student employment after taking this course has revealed that approximately 50% go to teachers' training college, 20% enter industry, the Civil Service, or hospitals, and 30% go on to post-graduate studies and research.

Because of the success of this course and the demand for students to learn more of environmental biology, the Department of Biological Sciences at Aston is planning in the near future to offer a full honours degree based on the existing Combined Honours course.

In spite of the success of the Combined Honours course it is felt there are many imperfections. For example, the syllabus is still somewhat fragmented, so that the emphasis on the interaction between man and his environment enabling the student to see man as a part of Nature may not yet have been anywhere near achieved. As a degree course very early in the field (perhaps prematurely) it needs improving. Perhaps the course should be taught as a technology for, whereas a science seeks to understand and interpret, a technology seeks to apply science and bring about change. If the Biology of Man and his Environment is to be relevant to the teaching of human ecology, then it should endeavour to be a technological course demonstrating biological technological advances, and providing the knowledge of how biological principles can better the relationship of man with his environment.

12

Degree Programme in Environmental Sciences at the University of East Anglia

J. R. TARRANT*

Aims

Over the last decade there has been an increased recognition of the breadth and complexity of environmental issues paralleled by a reaction of some students and faculty against narrow, research-orientated study and an appreciation of the connections between subject fields rather than the separation between them. The environmental crisis, if crisis it is, is the result of accelerating world population growth, where the populations involved are of rising economic sophistication, faced with a finite collection of world resources. The consequences of this confrontation is a shortage of world resources, pollution, and an awareness of pollution of the environment, destruction of wild life and landscape. If this does not lead to total destruction of the environment it leads to increasing dissatisfaction. There is some evidence that this culminates in stress and finally violence.

This is perhaps the general context of the growth of environmental education but it has given rise to a great variety of attempted education solutions. The diversity of interpretation placed upon environmental sciences, or studies, means that it is now usually necessary to define your terms before discussing the subject. The reasons for this variety of interpretations may be partly fortuitous, but in the case of the University of East Anglia, the nature of the course was partly the result of the constraints placed upon it by the existing framework of the University. In many ways, however, these constraints were less than might be expected because the University was recently founded without a traditional departmental structure firmly established. Environmental Science has grown in two distinct situations; in the new universities where there was no existing establishment to circumvent, and in existing educational establishments, often with a strong departmental structure, where interdisciplinary courses have been founded with more difficulty.

---

*The views expressed in this paper are those of the author and do not necessarily represent those of his colleagues at the University of East Anglia.

The scope of the School of Environmental Sciences at the University of East Anglia was determined by some four constraints:

(a) The original purpose of the University was to establish inter-disciplinary schools of study linking many traditional subjects. Departments do not exist and there is, for example, a School of European Studies linking language and literature. The reasons for this choice of structure were to enable this university to be different from existing institutions, partly to provide a different type of choice for potential students and partly so as to avoid duplicating the efforts of other, longer established, universities.

(b) The second constraint on the nature of the School was that of size. The policy of the university is to have relatively large schools, partly to enable efficient use of capital equipment and other facilities. The School of Environmental Sciences was planned to contain 300 students after an initial period with 150. There were two implications of this size. Firstly, there is the question of attracting a large number of students at a time when many subjects, more especially mathematics and physics, are finding the attraction of good quality applicants increasingly difficult. In this respect we could not afford to ignore the fact that geography remains a very popular 'A' level subject. We had to design a course which could attract part of this number. The second implication of size concerns the question of employment prospects for upwards of 100 graduates a year. Although many universities can be accused of conservatism in the recognition of new courses, employers as a whole are considerably worse. There could be little prospect of finding employment for our graduates if the course were in the nature of narrow specialisation, even if this had been desirable.

(c) Man should not be omitted from the study of the environment as the environmental 'problem' introduced earlier, concerns man either as a cause of, or a receiver of, this problem. The amalgam of man and the earth sciences brings a degree of purpose to the School. The current concern with the environment should be that there remains a world fit for man and yet adjusted to man, not a world fit for varieties of wild life and without man.

(d) The final constraint on the new School was the nature of the existing schools within the university. To some extent the problems evident here may appear to be a repetition of the problems of traditional departmental divisions but this is not the whole story. There was a deliberate policy from the start to reduce the emphasis on biology within the School. A part of the reason for this was certainly that there was already in existence a large School of Biological Sciences, but another, equally cogent reason was that we do not consider that the answers to world environmental problems have been, or indeed are likely to be found from within the field of ecology. Man's systems of organisation are very different from those of plants and animals both in scale and content. Despite the separations between Schools they are by no means insurmountable. Students may take courses in the School of Social Studies or in Mathematics and Physics and inter-school courses are to become considerably easier when the university adopts a common timetable.

In any academic study there is a conflict between breadth and depth. The education offered by an American liberal arts college contrasts with that available at an English university in this respect. Our course, as I outline below, is a compromise trying to avoid the label of teaching graduates to be "jack of all trades" without producing single subject specialists who would not be employable in the numbers we are teaching, and indeed would not fulfil the requirement of having a broad understanding of the environment in which they live and about which they need to be informed.

Before discussing the details of the course I should perhaps state the obvious; we are a young School undergoing a process of continuous development. We try to avoid the difficulties which come from an early fossilisation of a system which may not be suitable for later planned expansion. I try to describe the School in its present state of development indicating, where possible, future planned development. No doubt, as the School continues to grow to its full complement of 300 undergraduates, 40 graduate students and approximately 30 staff, changes and developments will continue.

Undergraduate intake

In common with most university departments we operate a three level process of admission selection; the university matriculation qualification; the special school requirements; and the selection by the School's admission committee of candidates to be offered places. I need not dwell upon the difficulties of reducing about 1500 applications to the number of conditional and unconditional offers necessary to exactly fill the number of places available, it is certainly one of the most difficult and time-consuming administrative problems we have to face. From 1968, when the School first admitted undergraduates, to 1971, fifty students a year entered. In 1972 this rises to 75 and in 1973 to 100.

The stipulation of special entry requirements for the School has given rise to considerable debate. During the course of his three years the undergraduate in Environmental Sciences will be required to achieve a level of competence in scientific method and in numerical and statistical methods. The extent to which this should be required of the applicants in the form of 'A' level science and mathematics, and the extent to which these can be provided during the course remains a matter of debate. Current requirements are for one of the 'A' level passes to be taken from biology, chemistry, geography, geology, mathematics, physics or physical science. In addition, a pass in mathematics should be held at 'O' level.

Assessment methods

As with so many aspects of the School, the method of assessment adopted is a compromise between two possible extremes, and, like many compromises, it has some of the disadvantages of both extremes. At the present time there are two examinations, one at the end of the preliminary programme to gain entry into the honours programme, and a final examination. In the near future this final examination will be replaced by a part one at the end of the second year and a part two at the end of the final year. These examinations make up between two thirds and one half of the total assessment. Throughout the teaching programme there is a method of course grading or continuous assessment. This is designed to reduce the pressures of a once and for all final examination and to provide a more broadly based assessment of the student's ability. In practice, by the retention of a major final examination, even though it does not count as much in total marks, the first of these objectives is hardly met, and continuous assessment has some detrimental effects on that work within the School which is not designed to be course graded. Nonetheless it is difficult to envisage a more satisfactory alternative system.

The Preliminary Programme

Given the breadth of the environmental sciences it is appropriate that a broad survey is provided in the first two terms. There are several advantages of this. The main function of the preliminary course is to introduce the undergraduates to as much of the range of environmental science as possible in order that they should have a base of knowledge on which to make their selection of courses for their honours programme. Much of the content of the preliminary programme will be very different from any 'A' level subject and this enables us to have a broadly based admissions policy and to allow some transfer of arts based 'A' level students to a science based course.

The preliminary programme consists of three parallel courses, two of which are made up of sections giving an introduction to many subjects within environmental science. Each course has three lectures a week, making six in all for the two environmental science courses. The third part of the preliminary course is called Methods and Techniques and is further divided into three. Two particular skills are required within many of the honours courses and in order to make the choice of honours options freely available to all students the preliminary programme has statistics and calculus and mechanics sections, making up two parts of the methods and techniques course. The statistics we regard as especially important and it is deliberately included at this early stage. While we, in common with most others with similar experience, find it hard to impress the concepts and applications of statistics to environmental problems on all students (especially as in most environmental examples the 'normal' distribution and all the statistics that are derived from it are inappropriate), we feel that some level of understanding in this field is essential. It is taught in the form of problem classes with the aid of electronic calculators and the university computer.

The final element of the methods and techniques course is an experimental one. We are concerned, not to make the students skilled in the operation of a series of laboratory techniques, but to introduce them to the problems of setting up experiments to measure environmental variables and to interpret their findings. These experimental situations cover a wide spectrum from an investigation of pedestrian movement to soil characteristics and variation. We concentrate on experimental design and upon observation and measurement. In addition to this practical course there are normal practical classes associated with both of the environmental science courses. In 1973 this preliminary programme is to be extended to three terms and it will then incorporate a wide range of experimental techniques which are at present taught in the form of service courses during the honours programme. These consist of advanced statistics, mathematics, computer programming and use, air-photo interpretation, methods of chemical analysis and surveying, with others which are added from time to time.

At the end of two terms, assuming success at the preliminary examination, students select three options to take in their second year and three in their third. Any one option is available to both second and third year students. These options are listed in Table 1 and are fairly self-explanatory.

Table 1. Honours Option Courses within the School of Environmental Sciences.

Applied Earth Science
Ecology and Palaeobiology
Economic Geography and Location Analysis
Geophysics and Earth Structure
Hydrology and Channel Morphology
Meteorology and Climatology
Oceanography
Quaternary Studies

Table 1 (continued)

> Rock Chemistry
> Soil Science
> Surface Processes
> Tropical Resources and Development
> Urban and Regional Planning
> Computing Science
> Mathematics

The two at the bottom of the list, computing science and mathematics, are available, outside our own School, for students who develop a special interest in an area of environmental science where these subjects are especially appropriate. In addition, other options are available outside the School in Social Studies although any great utilisation of these will have to await the adoption of a common university timetable. In order to limit the range of choice available, and to retain some integrity to the environmental science course, a student may take only one course outside the School during his honours programme.

The number of options available is limited and we do not envisage that this number will grow with School expansion. In fact it is about to contract by one with some re-combination within hydrology, quaternary studies, surface processes and applied earth science. The number of courses is limited for three reasons:

(a)   The first reason is a practical one, the shortage of laboratory space. Each option meets for six hours per week and this includes, usually, one practical class. There is not enough space on the timetable or in the building for more options.

(b)   The second reason is a consequence of the interdisciplinary nature of environmental science. We have tried to keep the options as interdisciplinary as possible. Oceanography, for example, is not divided into chemical and physical oceanography.

(c)   The third reason is related to the second, we feel that students should not be allowed to specialise beyond a certain level and should all have something of a unified course called environmental science. A proliferation of courses would make for a greater diversity of over-specialised graduates.

A further degree of flexibility is introduced into the honours programme by a third year option concentrating on applied, interdisciplinary seminar courses. After a three week introduction dealing with many economic and social questions including the allocation of external costs and benefits within the environment, the course divides into a selection of fifteen seminar courses, each of three weeks duration, from which list the students select five. The course ends with four weeks dealing with two out of four case studies. The seminar courses and case studies available this year are listed in Table 2. This course is designed to expand in the near future to include a more comprehensive list of

Table 2. Environmental Planning and Pollution Option

Seminar Courses
>Coastal erosion and protection
>Government and decision making
>Recreation demands and provision
>Flood perception, prediction and prevention
>Pollutant pathways in the ecosystem
>Radio-active pollution
>Water resource development
>National parks
>Atmospheric pollution
>Earthquake prediction, protection and modification
>Potential arable land resources of the world
>Principles of conservation
>Problems of planning and construction of roads
>The urban environment
>Applied aspects of oceanography

Case Studies
>The Tennessee Valley Authority
>The proposed Wash Barrage
>The Dutch Polder reclamation schemes
>The proposed development of Foulness

(The range of case studies is to be extended)

seminars and case studies. We rely to some extent on outside experts to contribute to many of these seminars and case studies, especially from the staff of the Fisheries Research Laboratory at Lowestoft.

The Project

We require a student project of about 10,000 words to be completed by the February of the final year. The regulations require that this should involve the collection, analysis and discussion of original data wherever this is possible. This project provides ten per cent of the final assessment. There are two problems associated with a project requirement of this nature; one, which is common to this type of work wherever it is operated, is the amount of supervision which can be made available to the student. This is an expression of a conflict between using the project as a teaching medium, where in some cases supervision may be highly desirable, and using it as a method of assessment where supervision has to be severly limited and standardised. The second problem is of more fundamental importance and concerns the relative difficulty of conducting a project in some fields of environmental science. How, for example, can students collect original oceanographic data? This problem is partly overcome by allowing the project to involve "raw" unanalysed data as is available from the population census or the daily weather records. There still remains a considerable imbalance in the number of students doing projects in the field of ecology or urban and regional planning in comparison with geophysics, oceanography or geochemistry.

Student demand/choice

Much has already been said on this question. We allow a free choice in the selection of option courses, partly because we are unable or unwilling to isolate desirable and necessary combinations of courses, and partly because we believe that free choice retains a high degree of student motivation. Nonetheless the free choice in conjunction with student demand has given rise to what is probably one of the greatest worries in the School at the moment. This is the very unequal balance of students choosing to do different options. The solution to this does not seem to lie in altering the admission requirements to the School because there is a genuine desire for science based students to take applied subjects. In order to balance the teaching load within the School it will be necessary to limit the numbers in each option to approximately 30, although this will double with the doubling of student numbers from 1973.

Employment

We are in no way providing a vocational training and we have placed graduates in a spread of careers not unusual to a more traditional geography and geology department. One year of graduates have embarked on further academic study in the fields of geophysics, oceanography, geochemistry, glacial geology, computer science, landscape design, engineering geology, hydrology and air-photo interpretation in planning. Teacher training has accounted for six graduates and three have gone into some form of town planning. Industry and public service accounts for fifteen. It is appropriate to restate that this pattern for placement would be more difficult, if not impossible for the numbers of graduates involved, in a more narrow, specialised school.

Conclusion

I have outlined the course we have developed at the University of East Anglia and, while being far from perfect, we hope the School achieved something of academic value while at the same time going some way towards satisfying a popular demand. We hope, however, that our foundations are stronger than those based on the popular demand of the moment. A more permanent stability is provided by a strong research base to the School, consisting of graduate students, faculty and research appointments, with considerable funding and equipment.

13

The Honour School
of Human Sciences in Oxford

E. PAGET

The need to remove the artificial limits to, and gaps between, many Arts and Science subjects has been apparent for some time, and more recently the affinities between the biological and social sciences in this context were discussed. Professor Pringle did so in his article "Biology as a Human Science"[1] in which, in addition to outlining the biological approaches to Human Science, he provides interesting and useful detail on the practical and academic evolution of the subject at Oxford. Mr. Halsey had also, in his Galton Lecture of 1967[2], approached the subject from a sociologist's viewpoint. These two were the principal proponents amongst a group of people from five faculties — Biological and Agricultural Sciences, Medicine, Social Studies, Anthropology and Geography and Psychological Studies — who held a prolonged series of meetings before presenting their specific proposals for approval by the University. It may be helpful to this conference to quote at some length part of the covering memorandum in the *Oxford University Gazette*[3] which accompanied the notice given by the Hebdomadal Council when it proposed to make a decree establishing the new Honour School, since it summarises succinctly the scope, content and justification for the inter-disciplinary study.

"The boundaries between many branches of biology, psychology, and the social sciences are becoming extremely tenuous, but development in these inter-disciplinary fields and a wider understanding of their importance is severely handicapped by the traditional definition of subject areas in university curricula and, particularly, by the continuing educational separation of the natural and social sciences. There are few, if any, who have professional competence on both sides of this division and even communication across it is limited. Areas such as the inter-relationships between human genetics and sociology; comparative social behaviour in man and animals; human ecology, demography, and social structure; and biological and social evolution are being neglected because there is so little understanding between biologists and social scientists. These fields are not only important academically but are of concern in practical human affairs; they are fundamental in considering, for example, problems in social selection systems, world population growth, and race relations. It can be said without exaggeration that almost all political, economic, and social policies have important biological, and especially genetic, implications, but these have largely gone unrecognised because of the lack of suitably trained people.

"The need to remedy the present situation is immediate. Some British universities are already starting to introduce special-purpose courses to improve inter-disciplinary communication. Elements of psychology and sociology are being introduced in medical education, and at the graduate level various attempts are being made to introduce sociologists to human genetics; but it is not possible in this country to obtain a basic education in the inter-related aspects of the social and natural sciences. It is just this type of training which is most needed, since only through it can there come people who will not only understand the methods, objectives, and attitudes of biologists and social scientists, but will also have professional competence to develop the inter-disciplinary fields".

Apart from academic justification however, practical considerations imposed considerable restraints on the precise form that the subject should initially take. The only practical possibility to achieving "take-off" at a time of extreme financial stringency, was to be able to assure the higher committees of the University that it would not entail a demand either for new academic posts or for new recurrent expenditure, and this was the major control on most aspects of the detailed composition of the School and on the numbers permitted to take it.

The syllabus was, therefore, perforce designed to draw almost entirely on existing courses of lectures and practical courses covering the biological and social aspects of the study of man, including the relevant elements of genetics, ethology, ecology, psychology, social geography, sociology and anthropology.

The subject is studied over three years with a *Preliminary Examination* at the end of the first year. This is not classified, but distinctions may be awarded. The four subjects are:

1.   General Biology
2.   Genetics and Evolution
3.   Sociology and Social Anthropology
4.   Geography[4] and Ethnology

Details of these subjects from the examination decrees, are included at Appendix A.

The Honour School is divided into two sections. All candidates offer six compulsory subjects:

1.   Animal Behaviour
2.   Human Genetics and Human Evolution
3.   Human Ecology

4. Demography and Population
5. Sociological and Social Anthropological Theory
6. General Essay.

Additionally, candidates offer two from five optional subjects:

7. Social, Developmental and Personal Psychology
8. Urban Geography
9. Modern Social Institutions
10. Social Anthropology
11. Advanced Quantitative Methods

Details from the examination decrees are given in Appendix B.

One was in a "cleft-stick" situation of being convinced of the basic unity of the subject, but obliged to present it as a series of so-called "fragments" or crumbs (from the rich men's tables of the recognised disciplines).

It seems clear from the subjects involved in this symposium (including as they do economics, architecture and planning and perhaps medicine to an extent not envisaged in the Oxford course), that the centre of gravity is somewhat different from those at other universities and undoubtedly this will be relevant to the particular aims and objects of the different courses.

But it may be helpful first to outline the reactions to the new School (as I saw them) within the University as a whole. They were varied and many "cancelled-out". Members of all Faculties were consulted. Two main and genuinely considered objections were apparent. One was that there was too much width and not enough depth; that students would "feather" over too wide a surface; that Oxford had excelled at teaching vigorously the (so-called) narrower conventional disciplines and that the newer Universities were adapted more suitably to multi-disciplinary courses. These objections were subscribing to the debatable viewpoint that more width and less depth is not academically respectable. A second reaction was very different. A number of cognate disciplines and subjects wondered why they had been omitted from the major group of subjects. Should, for example, climatology, etc., not be included in the study of man and his environment rather than tucked away as an incidental sub-section of one or two of the other papers? Such objections were, unwittingly perhaps, subscribing to the reality that all knowledge (*Scientia*) is one and indivisible.

I viewed the successive stages of acceptance of the scheme by the echelons of university committees with, I must admit, a sense of gratified surprise. The Secretary of the Undergraduate Studies Committee of the General Board of Faculties (a classicist by training) was asked to modify his reports so as not to refer to the proponents of the scheme as "a group of enthusiasts", when it was decided to recommend the scheme to the General Board of Faculties. The Vice-Chairman of the General Board, who was at that time an academic lawyer and is now

Head of one of the Colleges, is currently Chairman of the University's Standing Committee for Human Sciences, for it was realised that careful practical steering, organisation and particularly co-ordination was needed between the faculties concerned (Biological Sciences, Anthropology and Geography and Social Studies) and their individual lecturers and tutors. Lecture lists and timetables needed synchronising: lecture courses were scattered fairly widely and at some distance over the University area; likewise libraries, for which no central provision could be made. It has been possible to secure the use of a room fairly centrally located to act as a common room and seminar room.

Progressive efforts to improve the ways and means of integrating the course include the appointment of one tutor for each paper to act as liaison officer and give help to students on tutorial resources. Discussions take place both between Senior Members involved in teaching, and with the "consumers" (who are so far proving fairly durable!). A week-end discussion is also planned for lecturers and tutors to be based on a book entitled *The Structure of Human Populations*[5] since it offers a theme fairly central to the subject, covering demography, human genetics, social anthropology and human ecology, and will afford useful cross-fertilisation of ideas (if, in this context, that is an appropriate metaphor).

Colleges at the time gave generally a luke-warm reception to the proposals, but it is interesting that fourteen colleges have one or two candidates in the Honour School and three more which had not previously accepted candidates appear on the first-year list. Three of the women's colleges have candidates.

Colleges are not able to accept more candidates because of the operation of a strict quota system imposed by the University, restricting the numbers reading the subject to fifteen each year. Much ingenuity is required of the interviewing committee to balance the applications of freshmen with those from undergraduates who wish to transfer from other subjects. There has so far been a healthy balance between the two. Transfers are possible after two or three terms from such subjects as biology, P.P.E., and in some circumstances after passing the first B.M. in medicine[6]. The intention is to attract a wide variety of educational backgrounds, and no special entrance requirements are specified, except that all students are expected to acquire an adequate knowledge of mathematics, and there are compulsory questions on statistics in the Preliminary Examination; for this reason "A" level G.C.E. in maths and biology are useful but other subjects will be accepted in certain circumstances. Present indications are that the strict quota may be relaxed somewhat in view of demand, and new university lecturer posts have been secured in human biology and demography, with expectations of further possible reinforcements of teaching strength in biology in areas where tutorial and lecturing provision is at present restricted.

We were asked to consider the ends to which the Honour School is aimed — "employment prospects" — was the term used, and this must be a valid concern of everyone contemplating or taking the course. It is clear that the Oxford course is probably much less a specifically applied and vocational course than others described in this symposium, if the subjects listed are any indication.

The aim is essentially educational, to provide, as with other academic disciplines, a sound, logical approach to problems, but problems whose range is different from those normally encompassed by the traditional disciplines.

We were also asked to indicate the emphasis placed on each subject. Speaking as someone from one of the fringe subjects of this spectrum, I would suggest that the centre of gravity would appear to be in human ecology — not simply because it is listed in the centre of the compulsory subjects of the Honour School, but because it is central, between the micro-intensive (point) studies and the macro-extensive distributional studies. The official memorandum presenting the course referred to the need to study the relevant elements, ranging from genetics to anthropology and geography "in logical order". One aspect of this that is especially apparent to a geographer is the opportunity it offers students to study inter-related phenomena at different *scales* of magnitude and degrees of generalisation, ranging from the microscopic studies of cells right through to the macro-masses of large human urban societies. Problems of changes of scale are fundamental, for in general when the scale of study changes, the significant criteria change also.

The meeting points and integral nature of the subject have long been apparent to geographers who are accustomed to meeting the criticism of too much width and insufficient depth. For example, interest has increased recently in "perception geography" — the different ways in which individuals and groups perceive their environment and its resources; in the application of ecosystems to geographical method[7]; in the relevance of Darwinism to geographical thought[8]. It has also been helpful and salutary to compare the approach of the sociologist to migration[9].

But is all this so *new?* Oxford has had a Dr. Lee's Professor of Experimental Philosophy for centuries, and only last week I was reading a preliminary manuscript study on Professor H. J. Fleure by a research pupil, which he has allowed me to quote — "Fleure was inclined towards a bio-social concept of psychology, resolutely advocating that geography as the study of peoples and their environments must take into account the emotional and qualitative factors as well as the more directly economic ones. A fuller inclusion of bio-social psychology in geography would, he considered, be guaranteed if the discipline multiplied its contacts with anthropology"[10]

References and Notes
1   Pringle, J. W. S. (1969) *The Biologist,* vol. 17, No. 5.
2   Halsey, A. H. (1967) Sociology, Biology and Population Control.
3   *O.U.Gazette,* 7 August 1969.
4   Speaking as a Geographer, I feel that attention should be drawn here to the details of the syllabus in Appendix A which makes it clear that emphasis is placed on ecological, cultural and social geography and that we do not involve physical geographers direct.
5   Boyce, A. J. and Harrison, G. A. (eds.) *The Structure of Human Populations,* to be published by O.U.P. in 1972.
6   University of Oxford: Prospectus (1972-3).
7   Stoddart, D. R. (1965) Geography and the ecological approach, the ecosystem as a geographical principle and method, *Geography, 50,* 242-251.
     Stoddart, D. R. (1967) Organism and Ecosystem in Geographical Models, chapter 13 in *Models in Geography,* edited by R. T. Chorley and P. Haggett, Methuen, London.
8   Stoddart, D. R. (1966) Darwin's Impact on Geography, *Annals of the Association of American Geographers, 56,* 683-698.
9   Jackson, J. A. (ed.) *Migration,* Sociological Studies, 2, C.U.P., 1970.
10   Campbell, J. A. Mss.

Appendix A
The subjects of the Preliminary Examination in Human Sciences are:
(1)   General Biology
(2)   Genetics and Evolution
(3)   Sociology and Social Anthropology
(4)   Geography and Ethnology
Subject 1. General Biology
The cell as a unit of structure. Organization of the cell. Organs and tissues. Co-ordination. Embryology. Nervous system and sense organs.
Behaviour as an observable phenomenon; internal and external determinants; development and evolution. Animal communities.
One three-hour written paper will be set. There will also be a practical examination which will be assessed together with the practical work done by the candidates during their course of study.
Subject 2. Genetics and Evolution
Cells, chromosomes, and cell division. The nature and mode of action of the gene. Particulate inheritance, linkage, and crossing-over. Dominance, polymorphism and polygenic inheritance. Heredity and environment. Introduction to human genetics.
Evidence for evolution and elementary treatment of its mechanisms. Nature and origin of species. Adaptive radiation. Historical survey.

One three-hour written paper will be set, which will include one compulsory question on statistics (see below). There will also be a practical examination which will be assessed together with the practical work done by the candidates during their course of study.

Subject 3. *Sociology and Social Anthropology*
An elementary introduction to Social Anthropology and Sociology; their history, scope, methods, and bearing upon other subjects.

One three-hour written paper will be set, which will include one compulsory question on statistics (see below).

Subject 4. *Geography and Ethnology*

(a) *Geography*
: Geographical concepts of environmental influence and ecological relationships; factors in the development of cultural landscapes; patterns and types of settlement; geography of plural societies.

(b) *Ethnology*
The cultures and social institutions of selected peoples with special reference to their ecologies, economies, and spatial distributions.
One three-hour paper will be set.

Statistics
Frequency distribution and their summarization. The idea of probability. Elementary properties (without proof) of the binomial and normal distributions. The sampling distribution of the mean. Significance tests, including elementary analysis of variance, correlation, and regression. Sampling.

Appendix B. Honour School of Human Sciences
The Honour School is divided into two sections. All candidates will be required to offer the following six compulsory subjects:
   (1) Animal Behaviour
   (2) Human Genetics and Human Evolution
   (3) Human Ecology
   (4) Demography and population
   (5) Sociological and Social Anthropological Theory
   (6) General Essay
Candidates will also be required to offer any two of the following subjects:
   (7) Social, Developmental and Personality Psychology
   (8) Urban Geography
   (9) Modern Social Institutions
   (10) Social Anthropology
   (11) Advanced Quantitative Methods

Schedule of Subjects

1. Animal Behaviour

Description and analysis of animal behaviour; the basic questions (causation, survival value, ontogeny, genetics, and evolution); sensory equipment; complex stimuli; timing and orientation of behaviour; action sequences and their analysis; internal determinants and complex behaviour systems; conflict behaviour; social behaviour; the search for possible animal roots of human behaviour; "nature and nurture"; play and exploratory behaviour; development of social behaviour; animal language and human speech; aggression; genetic and cultural evolution.

Social behaviour in primates, particularly the study of organisation of social groups; relationships to ecological factors; reproductive and parental behaviour; communication systems; development of affectional systems; effects of early experience on adult behaviour.

2. Human Genetics and Human Evolution

The theory of genetic polymorphism; heterozygous advantage and the super-gene in man. Blood grouping. The simpler and the more complex blood group series. Other human polymorphism. Human sex-determination and sex-linkage. Heteroploidy in man. Multifactorial inheritance. Ionizing radiation and population genetics. Polymorphism, especially that of the blood groups, as a racial criterion in man.

Man's place in the Animal Kingdom; the order Primates; human palaeontology; general factors involved in the evolutionary emergence of man; the nature, genetics, distribution and selective significance of human characters which show geographical variation.

3. Human Ecology

The inter-relation between man and his environment. Population distribution in relation to habitat and economy; climatic, nutritional and disease ecologies; components of fertility; population growth, structure and migration; regulatory mechanisms of population size in animals and man; the role of man in changing his environment; conservation in natural resources; natural principles of land use.

4. Demography and Population

Population theories. Population statistics and projections. Quantitative methods in demography. Biological, psychological and social determinants of fertility. Causes of infertility. Ecological variance in death and birth rates. The age and sex ratio structure of populations. Historical demography. Causes and consequences of migration (international and national). World patterns of population growth. The geography of population distribution. Population control, family planning, and contraceptive technology. Evolution of occupational changes. City and metropolitan growth.

5. Sociological and Social Anthropological Theory

Sociological theory; the principal theoretical contributions to sociology, in particular theories relating to the social system; the sociological aspects of economic, political, religious, intellectual, and kinship institutions; social control; social disorganization; the analysis of social movements and organizations; social conflict; the processes of social change. Candidates will also be expected to show knowledge of the concepts and methods used by the principal writers.

Social anthropological theory: the history of anthropological theory; the theories of the nineteenth century; Durkheim and the school of *Année Sociologique;* structure and function; Malinowski, Radcliffe-Brown, and their successors; later developments; Evans-Pritchard, Levi-Strauss; Structural studies, theories of meaning, symbolism, systems of classification, belief.

6. *General Essay*

Candidates will be required to answer one from a range of questions, each of which will demand knowledge of more than one of the basic approaches to the study of human sciences.

7. *Social, Developmental, and Personality Psychology*

Person perception and social interaction; group processes, including norm-formation, decision processes, and leadership; role, status, and behaviour in social organizations; attitudes and attitude change; cross-cultural variations in social behaviour.

Changes of behaviour in infancy, childhood, and adolescence; origins of motor behaviour, perception, cognition and motivation; socialization and processes of social learning; the development of language; interpretation of developmental processes in terms of psychological theories.

Biological aspects of personality; inheritance and environment in relation to intelligence and other aspects of personality; the statistical analysis of traits and the assessment of personality; the analysis of personality in terms of learning theory, cognitive and verbal processes, and dynamic mechanisms.

8. *Urban Geography*

The historical background to urban growth; the influence of environmental and cultural factors on the evolution and form of urban centres; the planned town; principles underlying the distribution of cities; central place theory; methods of classifying cities; patterns of urbanization.

Land use in cities; the Central Business District; suburbs; the population of towns and its distribution within the urban area; the nature of transport in towns and the effect of transport on the urban plan; the evolution, form and functions of conurbations.

Candidates will be expected to show knowledge of the kind of maps useful in the analysis of urban areas.

9. *Modern Social Institutions*

Candidates will be expected to show knowledge of the following aspects of the social structure of urban-industrial societies; social stratification and mobility; demography and the family; urbanization; the sociology of industry and large-scale organization; the social context of politics; the social structure of religious organizations and of education. They must have knowledge primarily of modern British society but in the comparative context of other industrial societies. An understanding of modern techniques of social inquiry will be required.

10.   Social Anthropology

Candidates will be expected to show a knowledge of the major theories of the discipline. In addition they will be examined in more detail on: the anthropological aspects of population and demography, political systems, systems of marriage, alliance, descent (with their relation to and differentiation from their genetic and biological correlates), social development of the individual, the comparative study of political systems, theories of social control, theories of social change, linguistic and communication models, the analysis of belief, myth and ritual, symbolic representations, social anthropological methods and procedures.

11.   Advanced Quantitative Methods

General statistical principles and methods, including standard distributions, sampling properties and tests, regression and correlation theory, estimation methods, design and analysis of statistical experiments and sampling surveys.

Specific statistical and quantitative techniques discussed in relation to some fields of application in biology, medicine and sociology, including multivariate methods, analysis of genetic data, and demographic techniques.

Applications of stochastic models in the biological and human sciences.

Discussion of the papers of Mr. Carson, Professor Matty, Dr. Tarrant and Mr. Paget.

Dr. L. A. F. Heath, Plymouth Polytechnic. I was delighted with Mr. Paget's paper because in 1969, Plymouth Polytechnic put up a very similar course, entitled Bio-social Sciences, to the Department of Education and Science. We were told that the timing of such a degree was inappropriate, and I am pleased to see that this has not proved so.

With regard to Dr. Tarrant's paper, he said that students entered his course with a desire to "solve the world's problems" and that this had to be set aside for a while. I am a little worried at this and would hope that it might be avoided by attempting to use this desire by, for example, introducing simple problem solving.

J. R. Tarrant. It certainly does go against teaching experience to avoid utilising such enthusiasm. We do, in fact, require students to undertake problem solving, but we also try to make them appreciate that they will require considerable experience before they will have the capability of solving multivariate environmental problems.

M. J. L. Hussey. One way over this difficulty is to let the student tackle as big a problem as he likes and then to criticize his arguments, thereby ensuring that he realises the need for undertaking basic studies. If his motivation for basic studies stems, in this way, from his own experience, it may be more readily sustained when the relevance of his work is temporarily less immediately apparent.

Miss A. Coleman, King's College, London. Negative re-inforcement does not necessarily re-inforce motivation. It is better to set a problem which the student can solve. Otherwise, no matter how sympathetic one's criticism of an attempt at a complex problem, discouragement may result.

H. Bowen-Jones. To what extent do the speakers consider field work and vacation work to be of value in getting students out of the "classroom" situation and into "real-life" situations?

J. R. Tarrant. We have a field course element in the first year, and also what we consider to be a strong field element throughout the course. I would agree that it is field work which helps to bring home to students the complexities of the problems to be faced.

E. Paget. We find that a difficulty with the Human Sciences course which prevents extensive field work is lack of time. The amount of tutorial time necessary in the degree can be, for example, 50% higher than that for geography.

A. J. Matty. Whereas our Biological Sciences course has the traditional marine biology field course, the course on the Biology of Man and His Environment is based on the Swansea Valley and the students study this urban environment.

R. A. Eden, Huddersfield Polytechnic. Mr. Paget mentioned that "A" levels in Biology and Mathematics were desirable but not essential for the Human Sciences course. Does this mean that students may be accepted with "A" level Arts subjects?

If so, how do they fare on a science-based course such as this?

E. Paget. In fact, such a candidate is rather exceptional, and to date, most students have had at least some "A" level science background or have transferred from a science-based course such as PPP (Philosophy, Psychology and Physiology) for example, but we encourage a wide field.

M. J. L. Hussey. The use of computers can serve to make a great deal of mathematics unnecessary and thus reduce the difficulties of teaching students without previous knowledge of mathematics.

E. Paget. This is dependent on having adequate computing facilities and expertise.

J. R. Tarrant. In the course at the University of East Anglia we find that difficulties arise with statistics rather than mathematics.

14

The Technological Economics (Biology) Degree at Stirling

F. R. BRADBURY

Structure of the Course

The framework for the Technological Economics degree at the University of Stirling is shown in the Figure 1. It is based on the semester system adopted by the University of Stirling in which each year is divided into two sessions instead of the usual three. The degree occupies four years of which the first one and a half (three semesters) are devoted to Part I.

In Part I for Technological Economics, a student must take a science which may be chemistry, physics, biology or integrated science; he must take economics and he must take either industrial science or mathematics. The biology for technological economics with biology is the normal programme for a student taking biology in the university and the teaching is provided by the Department of Biology; likewise, the economics is the normal programme for an entering student and is taught by the Department of Economics. Industrial Science is a new subject, partly descriptive of how science and scientists are used in industry and partly a mathematical preparation for what follows in Part II.

At the completion of Part I, students may move in a variety of directions and are not constrained at this stage to go on to technological economics Part II. For those who do, the science is continued for a further three semesters and economics is continued right through to the end of the course. The economics in Part II becomes a selection from the wide field of possible economics teaching and falls within that which is usually described as management economics, being concerned partly with those parts of microeconomics such as production theory and price theory, which are particularly relevant to the industrial situation plus something on the behavioural theory of the firm and decision taking, these last being particularly relevant to the work of a practising technological economist in science-based industry. The industrial science in Part II becomes very much Stirling's own blend of management science, operational research and systems analysis; in fact, we often refer to it by the acronym ORSASEMSIS.

Figure 1. The framework for the Technological Economics degree, University of Stirling.

Semester	Subjects			Year
8	Project, Cases, Problems	technological economics		
7		industrial biology	man. econ. econometrics	4
6	biol.	indus. science	man. econ.	
5	biol.	indus. science	man. econ.	3
4	biol.	indus. science	man. econ.	
3	biol.		econ.	2
2	biol.	indus. science	econ.	
1	biol.	indus. science	econ.	1

Part II { spans semesters 7, 8 (top) and 4, 5, 6

Part I { spans semesters 1, 2, 3

In the fourth year of the Honours course, the contributions from economics and the natural science and industrial science are brought together in case studies, problem analysis and a project. Between the third and fourth year, there is a compulsory period of industrial training which is arranged between the university and industry.

Entry to the technological economics course requires the normal pattern of passes for entrance to a Scottish University with the inclusion of mathematics at 'A' level or Scottish Highers; there is no requirement for prior qualifications either in biology or economics.

Brief History of the Course
The origin of technological economics at Stirling was the recognition by the Academic Planning Board of the University of a gap between economics and technology. This gap is closed at the higher levels in industrial management by those who entered the business with science qualifications and learned their practical business economics on the way up. There exist, however, some serious gaps between appreciation of economics and of technology at lower levels in the graduate staff of science-based industry and this is matched by, and indeed stems from, a matching fault in the education programme for technologists entering industry. In universities and other higher education establishments, economics and technology (or the sciences on which technology is based) are separated from each other both philosophically (economics is usually taught paying scant attention to the process of technical change) and physically, by being housed in separate departments. This gap in teaching and practice is the more remarkable because of the importance of the area of overlap. This was recognised as long ago as 1959 by the Cambridge economist, W. E. G. Salter who, in his book entitled *Productivity and Technical Change* drew attention to the existence of a twilight zone where technological and economic factors interacted so strongly that to analyse problems in the area exclusively in terms of one or the other aspects was quite arbitrary. The Academic planners took the opportunity created by the new university to start work in a new subject area and wrote into the first prospectus the subject of Technological Economics.

Problems
Instituting an interdisiplinary course of this kind is not easy even in a new university. The problems encountered are of structure, integration, and student overloading. The problem of structure was attacked by careful selection from the field of economics those parts which are particularly relevant to the technologist in science-based industry and which have been referred to previously; there is a matching process of selection in the science topics — the biology scheme for example paying particular attention to the topic of today's meeting, human ecology, resource biology, and selected topics in systematic biology. The key step

in the structuring of the course was the identification of industrial science as a linking subject between economics and natural science.

Integration of the programme is achieved organisationally by the creation of a Board of Studies for Technological Economics which has the powers of defining the course structures, admitting students, appointing external examiners and the award of degrees. Perhaps the most important step in achieving integration is found in research in the interdisciplinary area and in the joint participation in teaching programmes and seminars where economists, industrial scientists and natural scientists make their contributions and participate in each others lectures and seminars.

There is a danger of overloading students in an interdisciplinary course of this kind because of the difficulty of persuading the contributing disciplines that they must sacrifice parts of their subjects which might reasonably be supposed to be indispensible. The history of the course has been a progressive elimination of some of the work-load. A particular aspect of this cropped up early in the course's history; the original intention was to have a combined honours degree in science and economics, but this was soon seen to be impracticable and the decision had to be taken whether to make the degree an honours economics with some acquaintance with science or vice versa. The former course was decided upon and that is why the science contribution to the honours course is confined to the first three years, after which the industrial science programme picks up the natural science and puts it into its appropriate industrial context.

Opportunities

There are great opportunities to profit from the successful overcoming of problems of integration. The Academic Planning Board of the University of Stirling recognised common ground between technology and economics. It cannot be denied that this exists in areas such as the contribution of technology to the production of wealth, the common use of money as a measure in many economic and technological analyses, the concern which both share with the future and the necessity to deal in their various ways with uncertainty, as well as a common language increasingly developed as a result of the use of computer programmes for modelling both economic and technological situations.

Despite this common ground, however, the most striking thing about the interaction of economics and the sciences on which technology is built are the conflicts between them. In very general terms these conflicts can be identified as stemming from the preoccupation of the natural scientist with small sectors of the larger problem area faced by economists; one might say that the natural scientist is a sub-systems man who enjoys the privilege of taking his problems into the laboratory whereas the economist deals with much larger systems and makes these manageable only by highly abstract models aided by that most convenient weapon *ceteris paribus.*

Another conflict in the approaches of the two disciplines is found in the preoccupation of the scientist and technologist with problem solving as opposed to the more discursive approach of the economist who often seeks to widen the agenda of consideration rather than move through the analysis to selection and implementation of a solution. The natural scientist is likely to accuse the economist of having opinions and to deplore the absence of an authoritative text on the subject. Research students coming to study for PhD and having a biology background find the conflicts that I have outlined above a difficulty, as indeed do some of their teachers. However, the rewards for coming to terms with these conflicting approaches both at the PhD level and at the under-graduate level are very great indeed. If we can educate men and women to help scientists use their precious talents selectively on those areas of the problems of the day which may be revealed by the broader analysis of the economist or other social scientist, we will have provided people who may contribute strongly to the problems of today and especially of tomorrow.

Industrial Science
The contribution of industrial science to the integration process has been referred to above. It is mentioned again here because the quantitative analysis provided by industrial science and its related subjects, along with the techniques of modelling and simulation are, we believe, essential weapons in bringing natural science and social science to bear on wide agenda problems such as those described in various papers at this Huddersfield symposium on human ecology. It is not without significance that the Pennsylvania school of Professor Russell Ackoff, a leader in the post war developments operation research, is now turning its attention to the problems of large systems and their interactions with people. A reading of the contributions to this symposium gives an impression, perhaps erroneous, that the contribution of quantitative methods and operational research approaches has not received the emphasis that it deserves in the educational programmes for those who would work in the fields of.human ecology.

Contributing Specialisms
I have noted from a number of the abstracts and especially from that of Mr. Gregson-Allcott's paper that there is some debate as to whether education for work in the vast areas which are encompassed by the term 'human ecology' should be of a very broad multi-disciplinary nature or whether the many problems which fall in this area could not be better tackled by contributory specialisms. I take the view that it is not very meaningful to educate on a programme so broad as to include something of everything which lies within the field of human ecology; rather I take

the view that education for work in this field should build on the potential impact of contributory specialisms. That is not to say that I support the monolithic single subject education which we have grown accustomed to, but I believe that a subject such as the one which concerns me at Stirling, technological economics, in which there is a main point of emphasis — in our case the emphasis being on the contribution of economics of the appropriate kind for dealing with problems in a science and a technology environment — will equip those so educated to make a significant contribution to the problem area under discussion. In other words, I would back the Stirling graduate in technological economics (biology) to make a significant contribution to many human ecology problems but I would not think of labelling him a 'human ecologist'.

15
Environmental Sciences at Plymouth Polytechnic

LEONARD A. F. HEATH

Introduction

If one accepts that the rapid changes of attitude and employment patterns now occurring are likely to continue, then one is forced to the paradoxical conclusion that educational establishments have a responsibility to try to educate students for jobs which do not yet exist. At present, a sixth former, aiming for a particular scientific career, must undertake up to seven years of study and research. At the end of that period he is trained for a job that may then no longer be available. During the nineteen sixties, there was a boom in Applied Biology courses, which trained pharmacologists, biochemists and microbiologists for the pharmaceutical industry. There are strong indications that this industry's requirements are now fulfilled, yet those courses still continue to produce such specialised graduates in quantities far in excess of those needed for replacement. Future courses must become less specifically job-orientated, and more concerned with the enhancement of general qualities such as intellectual curiosity, critical and analytical ability and value judgement. Allied with this should be training in the tools of these qualities, such as experimental method and statistical analysis.

A number of colleges have come this far, but still more is required. We must attempt to look forward to the period 1980 — 2010, which will be the major working period for our next few intakes of students; and ask outselves what then will be required for such scientists as we produce? If one is pessimistic, then it is possible to argue that all scientific education is a waste of time, and only training in survival under famine conditions is relevant to that period. Such an approach is assured of headlines, and has its value in turning public opinion towards favouring measures which should ensure the pessimists are proved wrong. Like Waterloo, it will be a close-run thing. The boom in gloom, however, is not the business of educational institutions. We have to be optimistic, and look towards the establishment of a human society in balance with its environment. Our job is to try to ensure that the intellectual and behavioural revolution required to achieve such a stable society, does not fail for lack of suitably educated manpower. This will be required not only in research, but also in the administration of the new society. Continuing research will be required into the structure and control of the ecosphere, into ever more sophisticated methods of recycling resources, into minimising pollution from industry and transport, and into food production and environmentally acceptable forms of pest control.

However, the greatest need will be for environmentally literate administrators, to devise and run an essentially scientific infrastructure for the new society. Environmental Sciences should replace the Arts and Humanities as a general educative subject for future administrators. It is fitted for this role, not only by its subject material, but also by its breadth and demand on numeracy. The very complexity of the environmental systems being studied should develop that flexibility of thought necessary (but alas, all too often lacking) in administrators.

In my department at Plymouth, therefore, we have decided to produce three degrees, all environmentally orientated. These are a B.Sc. in Biological Sciences, producing specialist biologists; a B.Sc. in Geosciences, producing geographers and geologists; and a B.Sc. in Environmental Sciences producing generalists who can interrelate and coordinate data emanating from widely different disciplines across the whole field.

B.Sc. Biological Sciences

This scheme has as its basic assumption, that organisms cannot be studied in isolation from their environment. The life process, after all, is essentially the organisation of parts of the environment into the material of living organisms. Environmental studies are therefore central to the scheme, and all students, regardless of whether they see themselves finally working in cell biology or ecology, are required to complete courses in general ecology and human ecology. Only outside of this may they specialise. This is in contrast to the majority of courses in biological sciences, where the study of the individual is central, and the study of its environmental relationships is placed as a specialist study. The basic structure of the Plymouth scheme is shown in diagram 1.

The specialist studies offered are clearly determined by our environmental philosophy. Each is concerned with areas where man plays a significant part in bringing about the modification of biological systems. Thus within cell biology special studies include such aspects as the reactions of cells to 'foreign' chemical substances, and to invading micro-organisms; while in the ecological option, special studies cover such areas as fish farming and pollution control. The most interesting aspect is probably "Modifications of Biological Systems", which tries to bring together systems usually studied separately by pharmacologists, biochemists and ecologists, and to interrelate them. Thus we study not only the effects and distribution of, say DDT, in an environment, but also its effect at organ and molecular level.

Diagram 1. Proposed Structure of B.Sc.(Hons.) Biological Sciences

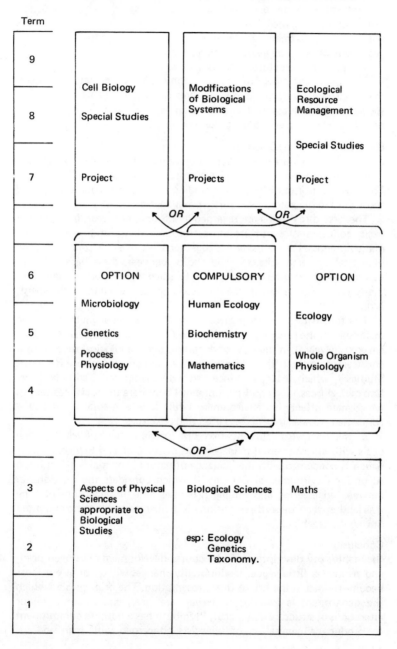

Term

9	Cell Biology	Modifications of Biological Systems	Ecological Resource Management
8	Special Studies		Special Studies
7	Project	Projects	Project

OR ↗ OR ↗

6	OPTION	COMPULSORY	OPTION
	Microbiology	Human Ecology	Ecology
5	Genetics	Biochemistry	
	Process Physiology	Mathematics	Whole Organism Physiology
4			

OR

3	Aspects of Physical Sciences appropriate to Biological Studies	Biological Sciences	Maths
2		esp: Ecology Genetics Taxonomy.	
1			

B.Sc. Geo-sciences
This scheme is planned eventually to produce geographers and geologists.
For reasons concerned with the possible rate of build-up of resources
within the department, this degree will initially confine itself to the
geography option, the geology being added later.
The probable structure is shown in diagram 2.

The important aspect of the geography is to concentrate on systematic environmental aspects, rather than on regional geography. Hence
special studies are planned in areas such as urban and rural geography,
population studies, economic geography and biogeography.

B.Sc. Environmental Sciences
Unlike the previously described courses, the aim here is to produce
generalists, and the approach is therefore consciously interdisciplinary.
This has led us into difficulties in finding titles for the course units, and
those used in diagram 3 need further explanation.

The first three terms are regarded as a foundation year, in which the
basic concepts of earth structure, resource distribution and mathematical methods are considered, together with relevant concepts in the
biological or earth sciences. The choice between these basic sciences
determines which wing of environmental sciences the student may eventually enter. The central concept — resource appraisal and management,
is open to all.

The fourth term is integrative, and will use seminar methods as the
major part of the teaching. It is concerned to examine the basic concepts
covered in year 1 in the light of economic and sociological theories and
constraints. In the fifth and sixth terms all students must take Resource
Studies I, which is largely concerned with the appraisal and classification of resources. Man and Environment I considers the social context in
which man affects his environment while Environmental Geology I is
concerned with earth processes affecting resources.

In the final year, students may opt for Resource Studies II, which
deals with environmental management, or for Man and Environment II
which is concerned with the "balance of nature" and man's effect upon
it; or for Environmental Geology II which considers the relationship
between engineering and mining processes and the environment. The
overlap between these three options is deliberate and is to be exploited
during the teaching.

Conclusion
Inevitably, my description of our course developments has been brief,
and perhaps a little vague. Undoubtedly changes will occur as our ideas
become refined in the fire of final presentation. The principles on which
the department is founded, however, are clear, and whatever minor
alterations of structure may occur, Plymouth has a definite commitment
to produce a generation of scientists concerned with man and his

Diagram 2. Proposed Structure of B.Sc.(Hons.) Geo-Sciences

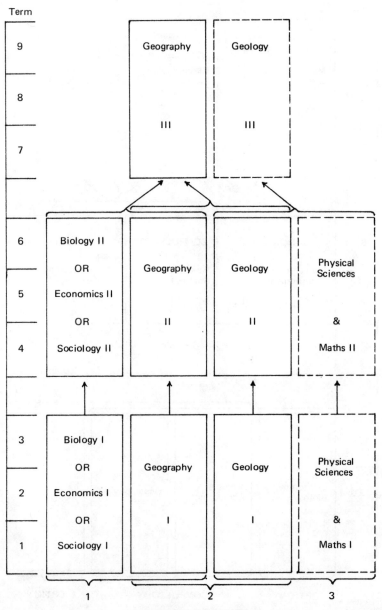

THREE OPTION GROUPS

Diagram 3. Proposed Structure of B.Sc.(Hons.) Environmental Sciences.

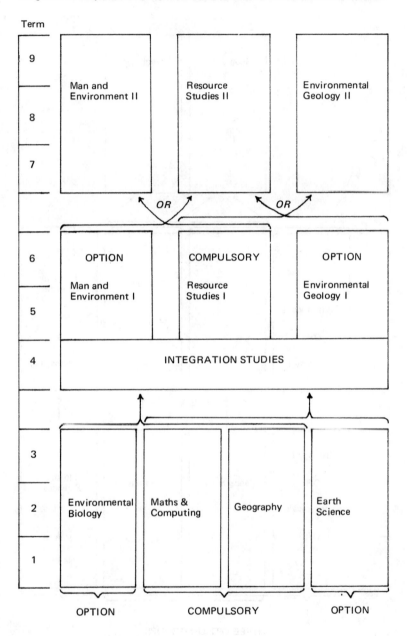

environment, rather than with the technology of industrial processes. Current student interest and demand for places indicates that a high proportion of that generation believes the course we are steering to be correct.

16

The Proposed Human Ecology Degree at Huddersfield Polytechnic

R. A. EDEN

Human Ecology is that branch of science which considers the complex of interrelationships existing between man and his biotic and physical environment. As a result of conditions such as pollution, competition, urbanisation and over-exploitation of natural resources the intensity of environmental stresses and strains within human communities is increasing and spreading. These stresses manifest themselves at two ecological levels:

    (a)   at the individual level, and
    (b)   at the community level.

The physiology of the individual is constantly adjusting to changing conditions in the immediate environment. Elaborate homeostatic mechanisms exist to maintain a dynamic equilibrium between the internal physiology of the individual and the condition of the habitat. If circumstances are such that the environment demands a degree of adjustment beyond the capabilities of the relevant physiological mechanism then steady state can no longer be maintained.

Each human ecological community consists of a complex of numerous species of animals and plants. Within this complex many factors both biotic and abiotic interact. Many animal and plant species supply man with food and other essential materials. Climate, altitude, soils and other features of the physical habitat interact with, influence and control the community in different ways, thus establishing a human ecosystem.

Within any ecosystem there exist regulatory mechanisms which maintain a dynamic balance among the several member species of the community, between the community as a whole and the constantly changing conditions of the physical environment.

Each human group has achieved considerable success in terms of survival and may have attained a high level of civilisation. However, no human society, no matter how complex or efficient its organisation, is totally self-sufficient, it must always operate as an integral part of a larger biological system, the ecosystem. Thus man manipulates, exploits, develops and conserves both his physical and biological environment. He has influenced greatly the mode of existance of those animals and plants with which he has become associated. Conversely, those animals and plants which live in particular geographical areas have had profound effects on man's welfare and distribution. Humans are both part of, and manipulators of, the ecosystem.

Whenever man alters his environment in order to overcome its limitations he is often faced with very undesirable consequences which are not easy to predict. I believe that a degree of irresponsibility about possible consequences does exist and that accidental changes are often disregarded.

Human communities are not static and may be assumed to be in a process of progressive or retrogressive evolution. Progressive evolution is occurring in many human communities: major improvements have been made in health and welfare, in new amenities for work and pleasure and in those regulating mechanisms which control the social and economic interrelationships within human society.

Retrogressive evolution has occurred in the past in many civilisations which once were dominant and is currently happening in many modern civilisations. It is difficult to list the causes of retrogression but possibly war, pollution, diseases, moral laxity and the over-exploitation of resources may be contributory factors.

Man has reduced and modified many of the natural and regulatory mechanisms operating within the human ecosystem. Disease, famine infant mortality are three mechanisms which play a less influential part in the control of human populations than they did centuries ago. Man, himself, must therefore take responsibilities for developing new mechanisms to maintain stability within his community.

New social, economic, political and biological mechanisms must be developed and existing ones constantly reviewed and improved. The successful development of new schemes will be facilitated only by increased communication between relevant disciplines and the creation of ecologists who by their training possess a comprehensive outlook towards man and his world.

Human autecology involves a study of human biology including anatomy, physiology and psychology. Community ecology overlaps the disciplines of anthropology, geography, botany, zoology, economics, sociology, geology and demography. The subjects of medicine, hygiene, agriculture and conservation must also be an integral part of any study of man and his environment.

Human Ecologists must therefore possess knowledge of that wide spectrum of subjects which form the study of human individual and community ecology. Close integration of these subjects is essential to help stimulate the development of a balanced and informed approach towards environmental problems.

Consequently the development of an Honours degree course in Human Ecology poses a number of problems.

The first criterion to be considered in a proposal for any new degree scheme is the definition of the aims and objectives of the course. These aims must then be converted into course "hardware" in terms of structure and content, resource requirements, both staffing and facilities, general timetabling and assessment procedures and the many other details required by the external examining body.

The main objectives of this course can be summarised:

1. To educate students of differing educational background.
2. To train graduates who:
    (a) possess a knowledge of the structure and behaviour of man and communities,
    (b) have an understanding of the structure, function and economics of the human environment,.
    (c) have an integrated approach to human society and associated environmental problems and are aware of the complex of interrelationships existing between man and his environment,
    (d) are seen to be well equipped for employment in industry, planning departments and those organisations concerned with environmental management and human relations.

The major difficulty has arisen in attempting to realise these objectives within the framework of a CNAA four years sandwich degree course.

Many obstacles are to be overcome for the successful development of a multi-disciplinary course. A degree of this nature involves crossing departmental lines, even institutional boundaries, and generating support beyond the parent institution.

The conventional, departmentally-orientated teaching and research programmes have often suppressed cross-fertilisation of ideas, and the close interaction of different disciplines and different faculties is both desirable and necessary for the successful development of this unique training programme.

Attention has been drawn to the many diverse subjects which impinge upon a study of human ecology. In drawing up a course structure it is necessary to rationalise these and to define major areas of study relevant to the aims and objectives of the course.

The course framework established is as follows:

Principal studies are in Human Biology, Ecology and Behavioural Studies.

Special optional subjects are Economics and Man, Systems and Landscapes.

The first year of the course involves a study of selected ancillary subjects. These include economics, geography, earth science, biological science, physical science and mathematics, the student's choice depending on his previous studies.

The problems posed in the first year of the course stem primarily from the different academic backgrounds of the students admitted. The entry qualifications as defined in the scheme require that the entrants to the course should hold passes in five GCE subjects of which two must be at advanced level. These flexible entrance requirements should attract an increasing number of school leavers with an interest in Human studies especially those who have studied both arts and science subjects to advanced level. However, the students who are admitted without an advanced level science qualification may immediately encounter difficulty with the Human Biology content. Their greatest difficulty is likely to arise in the course on Quantitative Studies where a proportion of students may recognise their inadequacy in mathematical studies and may actively resent statistical studies. To counteract the deficiencies in the science background of some entrants, balancing studies are provided in the form of ancillary courses. The student will select three ancillaries, their choice being determined to some degree by their previous background. The study of ancillary courses will be completed in one and one half terms. The time remaining in the first year is devoted to a study of Human Biology, Ecology and Quantitative Studies. Towards the end of the first year, students choose in consultation with their tutors the optional course which they would wish to pursue in their second and fourth years of study.

The second year of the course involves a study of three principal subjects, Human Biology, Ecology and Behavioural Studies. Economic Methods is taken by all students for one term only. This study will ensure that students who elect to take the "Man, Systems and Landscapes" option will have some basic knowledge of economic principles and methods to enable them to help quantify in economic terms certain environmental problems. The two special options are available for study in the second year and one is to be selected.

The optional subjects are intended to allow a student to specialise in one discipline. Obviously, in a multidisciplinary course the degree of specialisation cannot be equated with that of a single-subject special honours degree. This may lead to some criticism of the validity of the honours standard for this course. "Honours" can be justified and the whole standard of the course judged academically defensible, if it is understood that an essential feature of this degree is the development, by the individual student, of an integrated approach to human ecology. Whilst the prime responsibility for the development of this outlook rests with the student, every assistance will be given by the use of suitable teaching and study methods. These will include team teaching, seminars, tutorials and project work.

Structure of the B.Sc.(Hons.)(CNAA) degree in Human Ecology, The Polytechnic, Huddersfield.

Year	Standard Courses			Ancillaries
I Sept/Feb = 18 hours Feb/July = 16 hours including tutorials	HUMAN BIOLOGY 3 hours	ECOLOGY 3 hours	QUANTITATIVE STUDIES 2 hours	3 Courses from: Economics Geography Physical Science Earth Science Biological Science Mathematics 3 x 6 hours
II Sept/Dec = 20 hours including tutorials Dec/July = 20 hours including tutorials	HUMAN BIOLOGY 4/5 hours	ECOLOGY 4/5 hours	BEHAVIOURAL STUDIES 3 hours	ECONOMIC METHODS 3 hours SPECIAL OPTIONS (One to be selected) MAN, SYSTEMS AND LAND- SCAPES or ECONOMIC STUDIES 3/4 hours
III	INDUSTRY 12 MONTHS			
IV 16 hours including tutorials	ECOLOGY 6 hours		BEHAVIOURAL STUDIES 3 hours	MAN, SYSTEMS AND LAND- SCAPES or ECONOMIC STUDIES 3 hours
	PROJECT — 4 hours			

The third year of the course is spent entirely out of college. The students, dependent upon their choice of option, will be offered places in an appropriate industry or institution. Suitable sandwich places may be found in industrial concerns, in large planning departments and in those institutions involved with resource management and human relations.

The final year of the course includes a study of two principal subjects — Ecology and Behavioural Studies — together with the optional subject. A project is undertaken by each student in the final year. Where possible the project will be-related to the experience gained in industry. The function of the project will be to provide a practical example of the integration of ecological studies with either economic or behavioural studies in some aspect of the human environment. There will be considerable freedom in the formulation of projects, these will be chosen by the student in collaboration with a member of staff who will act as supervisor. The project will occupy the equivalent of 6—7 weeks' full-time study, and laboratory facilities will be available during the vacations for those undertaking projects involving experimental work.

The proposed Human Ecology Degree Course at Huddersfield Polytechnic represents a new venture in biological education. The range of subjects studied, coupled with specialisation will produce a graduate trained in both breadth and depth.

The process of subject integration, a vital component of this course, must be encouraged to proceed to such an extent that these graduates are "Human Ecologists". They are scientists trained in a unified discipline concerned with the human environment.

Discussion of the papers of Professor Bradbury, Dr. Heath and Mr. Eden.

L. A. F. Heath. I was struck by the similarity between the Huddersfield course and our own course, and would be interested to know why you call this human ecology rather than environmental sciences.
R. A. Eden. As we have seen during the symposium, one can make human ecology as broad or as narrow as one likes. Our problem has been what we can afford to leave out rather than what should go into the course. With regard to the use of the term "human ecology" as the title for the course, it is just a question of semantics, and we are, no doubt, speaking the same language.
Dr. S. Frost, Salford University. We should not forget about non-'A'-level education in human ecology, because students leaving school at 16 make up the great majority of the population. I was also worried about prospects for graduates of human ecology or environmental science courses, particularly where such courses are deliberately non-vocational.

L. A. F. Heath. I take the point that if you are running a non-vocational course you are producing a pool of people who do not have a direct vocational outlet. But this is not a new problem; classics graduates do not expect to get jobs in classics, they take the degree as a stage in their education. The present graduate employment situation has reached the stage where people can no longer get a job by waving a piece of paper. Graduates are likely to be employed partly on personal qualities and there is much to be said for the view that the un-employed graduate would be un-employed as a non-graduate as well!

F. R. Bradbury. We have both BA and MSc courses in Technological Economics but have not yet produced any graduates in the former course. Our experience is that prospects for those completing the MSc course are relatively good. In our own case at the BA level, the situation with students taking Chemistry as the science component of Technological Economics is eased by the fact that British Petroleum supports 12 students a year.

J. R. Tarrant. It is now very hard for graduates to get money to attend postgraduate courses. Either they must become more like American postgraduates and be prepared to work their way through postgraduate training, or, much more substantial government support has to be given to postgraduate professional training, otherwise many extremely valuable postgraduate courses are going to fold because they cannot get enough students.

F. R. Bradbury. There is a Science Research Council/Social Science Research Council committee which deliberately sets out to sponsor broadening postgraduate courses, and funding of such courses may be a lot easier than it is for straight science or social science courses.

P. J. Newbould. We tend to think of a three year first degree course as educational and a one year postgraduate course as vocational, but I think there is a strong case for two plus two arrangements.

R. A. Alexander, Napier College, Edinburgh. Although we have covered so many subjects at this symposium I would like to add another which has yet to be mentioned. Much of what happens to the human environment is due to our attitudes rather than to our knowledge and there should be room for the study of the history of philosophy, the history of man's attitudes. In addition, such a study would include a consideration of the scientific method and its development.

L. A. F. Heath. Our Environmental Sciences course is arranged on a modular basis and other modules can be attached to produce related degrees, one of which might eventually be in what may be called "the history of environmental philosophy".

P. J. Newbould. On a point of information, the New University of Ulster has a degree course in the History of Resource Management.

Conclusions

Following the formal symposium sessions, a series of workshops was arranged to enable participants to discuss matters raised during the symposium in greater depth than was possible during the plenary sessions. In view of the wide range of disciplines represented, it was not surprising that many different views were expressed during these workshops. What was remarkable was the measure of agreement reached on a number of general points. These may be summarised as follows:

1. While there was considerable variation in our understanding of the nature of human ecology a number of approaches were accepted as being generally valid. In view of this it would be wrong to expect a unity of approach in the many degree courses under development. Diversity was to be expected and welcomed.

2. At the same time, it was essential that information be available on the nature of new courses to avoid their developing in isolation. Following on from this symposium it was felt that an information centre was required, serving as a clearing house for information on developments in human environment studies. This should not be restricted to higher education but should extend to all levels.

3. Human ecology, with its holistic approach to the human environment, should be taught in schools and colleges at *all* levels, not necessarily as a discrete subject but more as an outlook or approach. This view was very strongly expressed by many participants, even though most were working in higher education institutions. The subject was far too important to be restricted to post 'O' and 'A' level students and the growing interest in environmental studies in primary, secondary and adult education deserved general support.

4. One particular area was identified as requiring special emphasis, namely the education of teachers. The development of the study of human ecology in colleges and departments of education, and especially by means of refresher courses for serving teachers, was probably the most important single action required in the immediate future.

157

Appendix

A Guide to Multidisciplinary Degree Courses concerned with the Human Environment

The third session of the symposium was concerned with degree courses in human ecology but shortage of time did not permit an examination of all the courses in progress or under development in the United Kingdom. The aim of this appendix is to present a more comprehensive guide and includes several courses for which details were not available at the time of the symposium. It is restricted to courses which include a study of ecology with a leaning towards human ecology but which also include the study of other disciplines concerned with the human environment.

UNIVERSITY OF ASTON IN BIRMINGHAM

The Biology of Man and His Environment

This course, described in detail in the symposium proceedings, may be taken as a one year Part 1 subject (together with two other sciences) or as one of two Part 2 subjects lasting two years in the BSc Combined Honours Degree at Aston.

In the Part 2 course emphasis is placed on those aspects of biology which have particular relevance to the study of man and his environment including population genetics, ecology, behaviour, nutrition, parasitology and social biology.

BIRMINGHAM UNIVERSITY

Biological Sciences and Geography

This is a three year course leading to the BSc Joint Honours degree in which selected aspects of the biological sciences and geography are studied with the purpose of providing a broad training in ecology and environmental sciences in the broadest sense, including their application to the problems of conservation.

BRADFORD UNIVERSITY

Environmental Science

The first students to this course will be admitted in 1973 and it will be a four year course with the third year spent in vocational training. The course aims to give students "an understanding of the physical nature and biological aspects of the environment and the processes which operate within it". It sets out to develop an appreciation of the human interactions with the environment with reference to resource utilisation and management.

The principal areas of study will be taken from the life sciences, geography and economics, together with a study of planning and managerial techniques.

CARDIFF UNIVERSITY COLLEGE

Interdepartmental Course on Environmental Studies

This course is a new development in the General Degree Scheme in the Faculty of Science at Cardiff. It will be taught, along with one other science subject, during the second year of the course and is intended to give an integrated view of the relevance of a number of science disciplines to the human environment.

Extensive use will be made of interdepartmental seminars and the course will involve the departments of Botany, Zoology, Geology, Microbiology, Biochemistry, Chemistry, Archaeology and Mineral Exploitation. The course is seen as an interim development which is likely to expand in future years.

UNIVERSITY OF EAST ANGLIA

Environmental Sciences

This honours degree programme is offered by the School of Enviorn-mental Sciences, the aim of which is to "draw together the relevant parts of the disciplines of geography and geology, together with the related subjects of geophysics, oceanography, meteorology, hydrology, soil science, ecology and planning, in the study of the environment".

Although largely concerned with the physical environment the three year degree programme includes introductory lectures on such subjects as the location of economic activity and ecology. At a later stage in the programme options are available in subjects including ecology, hydrology, oceanography, soil science, tropical resources and develop-ment and urban and regional planning.

EXETER UNIVERSITY

Environmental Chemical Engineering

This new course, commencing in October 1973, will lead to a BSc Honours degree and aims to produce engineers who will be acceptable as full corporate members of the Institute of Chemical Engineers. Their training will help them to apply the basic concepts and intellectual skills of chemical engineering to the solution of problems which affect the environment and the course will involve an integration of basic chemical engineering with aspects of biology, geography, geology and meteorology.

The subject is interdisciplinary and "embraces, on the one hand, pollution and its control and the underlying biological, hydrological and meteorological science involved in understanding its effects, and on the other, the management of natural resources, conservation, and the recovery and re-use of materials, particularly those potentially in short supply, that are at present wastefully and damagingly discarded by civilisation".

HUDDERSFIELD POLYTECHNIC

Human Ecology

The proposed programme is planned to start in 1974 and will be a four year sandwich course, students spending the third year in relevant employment. Core subjects are ecology, human biology, behavioural studies and economic methods. Two major options will be available; systems geography and economics.

KEELE UNIVERSITY

Biology and Economics

In the BA (Honours) programme at Keele, students on the four year course take a foundation year covering a wide range of subjects, and, following successful completion of this year, students are admitted to a Principal course of three years' duration in two subjects.

Subjects which may be studied along with biology include economics, geography, psychology and sociology, and as the biology course can include detailed studies in ecology Keele is one of the few universities in Britain in which it is possible to study ecology along with economics or sociology.

Students taking the biology course are given a basic course for six terms followed by an advanced course lasting two terms, the advanced courses available including one in ecology and evolution. This involves the study of plant and animal ecology, including physiological ecology, and animal behaviour; evolutionary genetics and one special topic.

The third year of the economics course can include special studies in international economics and economic development, and that of the sociology course can include medical sociology and social anthropology.

Although there is no integrated course in human ecology at Keele, it is therefore possible for students to take a course covering many aspects of human ecology.

LANCASTER UNIVERSITY

Environmental Sciences

The BA Honours degree course in Environmental Sciences at Lancaster aims to provide a course for those wishing to acquire an appreciation of the physical environment. Even so it includes components of a rather wider nature. For example in the first year, lecture courses in "Problems of Environmental Management" are available, and third year courses in pollution and also water resources management are offered.

LEICESTER UNIVERSITY

Combined Studies

Included in the wide variety of subject combinations available in the combined studies programme are biological sciences, geography, economics and sociology.

As part of this programme a new subject will be available from 1973, this being a one year supplementary course in Environmental Studies (Water Resources). Although taught by the Department of Engineering it will involve the co-operation of the Department of Economics and the School of Biological Sciences. According to the prospectus "it will take a broad view of an important feature of the interaction between man and his environment by examining in detail the engineering, economic and ecological aspects of problems related to the management of water resources".

NORTH LONDON POLYTECHNIC

BSc Honours Geography

This new course, commencing in 1972 is concerned with Geography as Human Ecology and is claimed to have no close parallel anywhere in Britain. It has been designed to provide an academically rigorous course of tertiary education in the geography of the human environment.

Following a two-term introductory course all students take a four-term main course which can include studies in environmental management, economic studies and ecology. In the final year of this three year course students study the nature and growth of planning in Britain and are given a selective treatment of environmental problems in Britain on a regional and local planning level. A wide range of short optional courses is available and students also complete a dissertation.

OXFORD UNIVERSITY

Human Sciences

This honour school involves the study of aspects of biology, geography and the social sciences and is intended to provide an integrated pattern of education in the biological and social aspects of the study of man. Courses available include human genetics, population studies, physical and social anthropology, human ecology, social psychology, sociology and urban geography.

PLYMOUTH POLYTECHNIC

Environmental Sciences

The three year course leading to a BSc honours degree is consciously interdisciplinary and is intended to produce graduates who can co-ordinate and interrelate data from widely differing disciplines. In the final year some specialisation is possible, with students opting for courses in environmental management, environmental geology or human ecology.

The course is planned to commence in 1973.

SALFORD UNIVERSITY

Environmental Sciences

This course is rather different from other environmental science courses, being offered primarily by the Departments of Civil Engineering and of Sociology, Government and Administration.

The course does, however, include aspects of biology and geography and has as its aim "a study of those aspects of the environment, especially the urban environment, in which there lie hazards to the health, safety and welfare of society, and of the legal and administrative means by which such hazards may be controlled".

SHEFFIELD UNIVERSITY

Natural Environmental Science

This is a new Special Honours Degree course, starting in 1973, which involves the collaboration of the Departments of Botany, Geography and Geology. The curriculum includes the study of natural ecosystems and primary productivity on both land and sea, climatology, geomorphology and geochemistry, natural resources, hydrology and economic geology. Advanced options will be available in the final year and a general aim of the course will be to foster the management approach to natural resources.

Natural Environmental Science with Landscape Studies

This course leads to a combined honours degree and is intended for those students who wish to study in depth the management aspects of the natural environment. It involves studies in aspects of botany, geography, geology and landscape architecture in the first two years followed by studies in ecology and landscape architecture in the third year which will include such topics as pollution, plant tolerance and land reclamation together with rural and recreation planning. Provision will be made for students to proceed to a fourth year of study in order to gain a professional qualification.

SOUTHAMPTON UNIVERSITY

Environmental Sciences

This is an interdepartmental course involving the Departments of Biology, Geography, Geology and Oceanography and leads to the degree of BSc Honours. It aims at a scientific study of the interactions of the various components of man's natural environment. A flexible unit system allows for individual bias on the part of students in the latter part of the three year course. Possible specialisations in the final year include plant and animal ecology, aspects of economic biology and resource management and conservation.

Economics with Ecology

A new programme allows students to combine honours degree level studies in economics with a major option in ecology. The option, Environmental Economics and Ecology, is intended to train economists to an appreciation of the further dimensions of the economic problems that arise in connection with the environment and who, in conjunction with specialists from other fields, can make progress in the analysis of total environmental problems.

STIRLING UNIVERSITY

Technological Economics (Biology)

This is one of several related degree programmes which are intended to bridge the gap between technology and economics. The main subjects for study are economics, industrial science and biology, with the latter including a component of human ecology which includes studies in population ecology, physiological ecology and ecosystem ecology of man.

UNIVERSITY OF STRATHCLYDE

Environmental Engineering

Although this course has a relatively small emphasis on ecology it is considered to be a pioneer course in its attempt to study the application of engineering and biological science to the control of people's physical surroundings. It is a four year programme, the first year being typical of many engineering courses. In the second and third years students study aspects of mechanical engineering and mathematics along with environmental engineering and biology. In the honours programme the final year is spent in studying either biological science with emphasis on environmental hygiene or engineering and physical aspects of environmental control.

NEW UNIVERSITY OF ULSTER

Three degree programmes are relevant to the present survey.

Environmental Science

This adopts an interdisciplinary approach with related studies in biology and physical geography forming the core of the programme. The provision of optional courses enables a student to orientate his studies to either ecology or planning, the wide range of courses including biogeography, conservation, water resource studies, systems analysis in environmental science, and population ecology.

Human Ecology

This is the only full degree programme in human ecology available in Britain at the time of writing. Human ecology is here considered to be the "study of the complex of interrelationships whereby human populations co-exist with other species in the physical context of nature". It is presented as a single subject programme by a panel of teachers specialising in biology, geography and social anthropology and sociology.

History of Resource Management

This unique course attempts to provide an understanding of man's use and management of his resources concentrating on the past 200 years. It also analyses present attempts to utilise resources and to conserve the environment in the future. The course therefore embraces history, especially economic history, geography, especially human geography, and aspects of biology relating to ecology and conservation. It is a BA programme whereas the other courses lead to the BSc degree.

WYE COLLEGE — LONDON UNIVERSITY

Rural Environment Studies

This BSc Honours degree aims to provide a comprehensive training in the natural, social and economic aspects of land use and conservation, being mainly concerned with the inter-action between man and the rural aspects of his environment.

The three year programme covers a wide range of studies including ecology, economics, conservation, environmental pollution and land-scape planning and management.